JEZEBEL AND THE BATTLE FOR AMERICA

Vaughn Martin

JEZEBEL AND THE BATTLE FOR AMERICA

Vaughn Martin

ISBN: 0-9787875-9-5

ISBN-13: 978-0-9787875-9-2

CONTENTS

ABOUT THE AUTHOR

Vaughn Martin is the founder of Overcomers Mission Schools, which train missionaries from a gamut of people groups for effective service in different parts of the world. He is author of *Open Heavens: A Biblical Guide to High-Level Spiritual Warfare* and other biblical and missiological titles. In this book, Vaughn applies the lessons he has learned on the mission field to the spiritual battle taking place for America today.

INTRODUCTION

America is facing a spiritual battle greater than any she has faced in her history. The outcome of this battle will determine the future of this great nation.

Most people are aware of the deep divisions and building turmoil in our nation. But behind the political struggles, a hidden battle is taking place for the soul and future of America. Sometimes the veil into this unseen spiritual arena is lifted a bit, and we catch a brief glimpse of the spiritual battle raging for our nation.

In 2008, Barack Obama was preparing to receive the Democratic Party's presidential nomination. As the primary campaign was winding down, Obama insisted on traveling to Berlin, where he wanted to give a speech at the Brandenburg Gate, part of the Berlin Wall separating east and west Berlin during the Cold War. This caused consternation among German politicians since the Brandenburg gate held great symbolic significance for the Germans. It was the place where Ronald Reagan gave the speech in which he said, "Mr. Gorbachev, tear down this wall!"

Since the fall of the Soviet Union, this gate had come to symbolize the unity of Germany and the unity of Europe. It didn't seem proper for a mere political candidate to give a speech there. So Obama ended up giving his speech to two hundred thousand people in a park located about a mile from the gate.

I have a friend, John Harris, who is very prophetically gifted. He told me, "When Obama gave that speech in Berlin, I received a vision from God where I saw Obama seating himself on Satan's throne."

This seemed like a very odd piece of revelation. I didn't agree with Obama politically on many things, but to claim he was sitting on Satan's throne and using satanic authority seemed a stretch. But as I looked more closely into the matter, I became convinced there was something to John's revelation.

Satan's throne is described just once in the Bible in Revelation 2:13, part of a message Jesus gave to the church in the city of Pergamum, located in present day Turkey: "I know your works and where you dwell, where Satan's throne is." Many scholars agree this is a reference to the "Great Altar of Zeus," constructed by the ancient Greeks in Pergamum. This massive altar was thirty-five meters wide by thirty-three meters deep with carved marble sculptures on each side depicting a war between the gods. A double row of Greek pillars formed a squared horseshoe shape around the center of the altar, while in the front an expansive set of stairs led to the ground. For hundreds of years, sacrifices to Zeus, the king of the false gods of Greece, were made on this altar.

During the late nineteenth century, German archaeologists received permission from the Ottoman Empire authorities to move the Pergamum altar to Berlin. The altar and its marble relief panels were shipped to Berlin, where they were reconstructed to become the centerpiece of the Pergamum Museum, opened in 1930.

In his book *Inside the Third Reich*, Nazi architect Albert Speer admits that the Pergamum altar provided him with inspiration for the architectural design of the Zeppelin Field where the Nazi party rallied and Hitler reviewed his troops. The Zeppelin field has rows of pillars, and the steps of the grandstand lead up to the center of the "altar" where Hitler stood.

The devil is always looking for ways to connect humanity to his authority and rulership. One way he does this is by convincing people to use symbols that represent him in some way. These symbols give the legal "right" to rule over the one who uses them. For example, if you tattoo yourself with a picture of a fallen angel or a symbol of death, this gives the one who robs, steals, and destroys the legal right to afflict your life. When the Nazis modeled one of their central pieces of architecture after Satan's throne with Hitler standing in the middle of it, this revealed a high-level connection between the Nazis and Satan himself.

When John told me he had a vision of Obama sitting on Satan's throne as he gave his speech near the Brandenburg Gate, he didn't know that Satan's throne was located right down the street. What happened next shocked me. Obama returned to the United States to receive the Democratic Party's nomination for the 2008 presidential election. The ceremony was to be held at Invesco field, home of the Denver Broncos football team.

There in the center of Invesco Field, a rather strange-looking structure was built. It was a stage similar to those football arenas use for rock concerts. On the stage was something that resembled a Greek temple. A double row of Greek pillars in a horseshoe shape lined the rear and both sides of the stage, surrounding the central stage where Obama's podium was located. An expansive set of stairs led down from the podium to the ground.

Political commentators wondered why Obama was building such a structure. Some right-wing commentators wondered if he thought he was a Greek god. The reality was much worse. The Democrats had built a stylized replica of the Pergamum altar in the center of that stadium.

John believes that when Obama received the Democratic nomination from this platform, the Democratic Party was dedicated to satanic forces, forming high-level connections with the rulers of darkness. And in fact, there seems to have been a drastic change in the Democratic Party. It is no longer the political party I supported when I was a young man. It seems to have become a party without restraint controlled by radicals who give full-throated support to the great evils of our day, including abortion, sexual perversion, and the eroding of our constitutional rights.

The point of this story is not to condemn a single political party. Political leaders on both sides of the political divide have aligned themselves with forces of darkness. Connections are being made and plans laid to destroy everything that is good and godly in our land. Evil spiritual forces are working behind the scenes to bring our nation into bondage.

In this book, I am going to describe the spiritual battle that is taking place for America. Out of all of Satan's forces, out of all of America's enemies, there is one more dangerous than any other. Her name is Jezebel. The spirit of Jezebel is the enemy of true freedom and the enemy of America. In this book, we will study the ways in which the spirit of Jezebel is working to enslave America as she builds a governmental and religious system that will eradicate true freedom in our land.

We will also study how this spirit will be defeated. If we understand our enemy, we can defeat our enemy. The ancient Chinese master of warfare, Sun Tzu wrote in his book *The Art of War*:

> *If you know the enemy and know yourself, you need not fear the result of a hundred battles. If you know yourself but not the enemy, for every victory gained you will also suffer a defeat. If you know neither the enemy nor yourself, you will succumb in every battle.*

In this book, we will try to understand our enemy, who cloaks everything she does in a veil of darkness and lies. If we understand America's enemy, we can understand how she can be defeated. And if we understand who we are and who Christ is in us, we will win the spiritual battle for this nation.

Chapter One

WHO IS JEZEBEL?

In the book of Revelation, Jesus appears to John the apostle in a vision and gives him messages for the seven churches of Asia. To the church of Thyatira, located in present-day Turkey, Jesus speaks the following message.

> *These are the words of the Son of God, whose eyes are like blazing fire and whose feet are like burnished bronze. I know your deeds, your love and faith, your service and perseverance, and that you are now doing more than you did at first. Nevertheless, I have this against you: You tolerate that woman Jezebel, who calls herself a prophet. By her teaching she misleads my servants into sexual immorality and the eating of food sacrificed to idols. I have given her time to repent of her immorality, but she is unwilling. So I will cast her on a bed of suffering, and I will make those who commit adultery with her suffer intensely, unless they repent of her ways. I will strike her children dead. Then all the churches will know that I am he who searches hearts and minds, and I will repay each of you according to your deeds. (Revelation 2:18-23 NASB)*

Of the seven churches described in Revelation, the church of Thyatira is most similar to the American church at this time. The Lord praises this church for her works, love, service, faith, and patience. Likewise, the church in America has done some great works, working to spread the gospel of Jesus Christ through the nations. The American church has emphasized the love of God and the power of faith, similar to the church of Thyatira.

But the church of Thyatira also tolerated "that woman Jezebel" and allowed her to minister to the people. Who is this woman Jezebel Jesus is speaking about who teaches, prophesies, and seduces the people? She is leading the church into sexual immorality and idolatry. Jesus promises that His judgment upon her and her offspring will be very severe. Jezebel and those who participate in her immorality will suffer greatly if they don't repent. Her children will be put to death.

Of all the books of the Bible, the book of Revelation uses symbolism the most. This "woman Jezebel" Jesus speaks about is not a human being, though she works with and through human beings. Jezebel is an evil spiritual being, a deceiver who brings the people of God into sin and captivity. Writing to the church of Ephesus, the apostle Paul told them that their real enemy was not people but evil rulers seated in the heavenly realms, ruling over the earth.

> *For we do not wrestle against flesh and blood, but against principalities, against powers, against the rulers of the darkness of this age, against spiritual hosts of wickedness in the heavenly places. (Ephesians 6:12 NKJV)*

The Bible speaks repeatedly of powerful spiritual beings who are in rebellion against God. Many people refer to these beings as fallen angels. The Bible often doesn't describe their exact nature but refers to them as princes, rulers, even gods, as well as angels. These beings serve under the authority of the devil himself, who is called "the god of this world" (2 Corinthians 4:4).

These "rulers of darkness" are high-ranking spiritual beings who rebelled against God and who work to keep the world in spiritual darkness, separating people from the God who created them. It seems clear that Jezebel is one of these evil spiritual beings. In particular, Jezebel is an evil spiritual being who is able to infiltrate churches, teaching them the ways of darkness and bringing them into spiritual bondage. In this book, we will refer to this spiritual being as the spirit of Jezebel, or a Jezebel spirit.

This spirit is not a woman. It does not have a physical female body with female body parts. Nevertheless, the Bible always uses feminine imagery and pronouns when it refers to this spirit. So in this book I will typically refer to this spiritual being as "she."

Also, this spirit can use and control men and women, but it more commonly attempts to use women as its vehicle for accomplishing its purposes. It is skilled in twisting and perverting the God-given nature and characteristics of women so that they work in unity with its purposes.

This Jezebel spirit and those who work in unity with this spirit usually work behind the scenes, controlling and manipulating the figureheads of authority in a nation or other organization, who are often male. Jezebel is the puppet master, pulling the strings of her marionettes, ensuring that everyone dances to her tune. She works together with compliant authority figures who come under her control.

This spirit pretends to support women's rights and freedom. In fact, this spirit is the enemy of everything that is feminine, everything that is good and valuable in women. It is the enemy of every quality and gift that has been given to women. It despises and devalues women's most precious works, qualities, and God-given strengths.

In chapter 13, we will discuss the differences between the strong, noble, and godly woman of Proverbs 31 and the bitter, wounded, and manipulative women who work in union with Jezebel. It is the noble woman of Proverbs 31 who manifests the true calling and dignity that God has given to women. She is the greatest enemy of Jezebel because she exposes the lies and evil nature of this spirit.

THE BIBLICAL QUEEN JEZEBEL

Jezebel was the name of a queen who ruled over Israel with her husband Ahab about eight hundred fifty years before the time of Christ. In studying the life of this queen, we can learn much about the spirit of Jezebel that Jesus spoke about. We first read about Jezebel and her husband King Ahab in the Old Testament chronicles of the kings of Israel.

> *In the thirty-eighth year of Asa king of Judah, Ahab the son of Omri became king over Israel; and Ahab the son of Omri reigned over Israel in Samaria twenty-two years. Now Ahab the son of Omri did evil in the sight of the LORD, more than all who were before him. And it came to pass, as though it had been a trivial thing for him to walk in the sins of Jeroboam the son of Nebat, that he took as wife Jezebel the daughter of Ethbaal, king of the Sidonians; and he went and served Baal and worshiped him. Then he set up an altar for Baal in the temple of Baal, which he had built in Samaria. And Ahab made a wooden image. Ahab did more to provoke the LORD God of Israel to anger than all the kings of Israel who were before him. (1 Kings 16: 29-33, NKJV)*

From this passage, we learn that Jezebel was a Sidonian, the name the Bible uses for the Phoenicians. King Ahab's father Omri had formed a friendship with the Phoenicians as he established his control over the northern kingdom of Israel, which by this time had broken away from the southern kingdom of Judah, still ruled by the descendants of King David. The northern kingdom's capital was in the city of Samaria.

By marrying Jezebel, daughter of King Ethbaal of the Sidonians, King Ahab had gone even further than his father in his connections with the Phoenicians and their idolatry. The Phoenicians were famous in the ancient world for their dedication to Baal and other false gods, whom they worshiped with child sacrifices. Phoenician parents would sacrifice their own children to these gods.

According to the first century Roman-Jewish historian Josephus, the bronze idols of Baal were constructed with outstretched hands projecting over a fire. Babies were placed into the bronze hands of the idol so that the child was held over the fire and burned alive. The ashes of these child sacrifices were then placed into clay urns, which were buried in child cemeteries known as tophets. Above the urns, parents inscribed dedications to their gods on stone tablets, thanking them for hearing their prayers and blessing them.

Archeological scholars have doubted the reality of child sacrifice among the Phoenicians. In the 1970s, scholars speculated that these accusations were merely anti-Phoenician propaganda propagated by their enemies, the Greeks and Romans. But in more recent decades, modern scholars have come to accept the reality of this large-scale child sacrifice. A number of Phoenician child cemeteries have been discovered providing irrefutable evidence of the practice. In a single tophet discovered in Carthage, the ashes of twenty thousand babies were found in clay urns, complete with stone tablets thanking the gods. On a typical tablet associated with a child's ashes, a parent thanks Baal for having "heard my voice and blessed me."

This was the religion of the Phoenicians, the religion of Jezebel. When Jezebel married Ahab and moved to the northern kingdom of Israel, she brought her religion with her. Ahab constructed a temple for Jezebel in his capital city of Samaria so she could continue worshiping Baal. In addition to serving Baal, Jezebel was also a worshiper of Asherah, the mother goddess of the Phoenicians. The Sidonians believed that Asherah was the partner or lover of El, their supreme god, and the mother of seventy lesser gods.

Asherah was a fertility goddess. "Asherah" poles were erected next to the altars where Asherah was worshipped, probably as symbols of the human penis. Sacred groves of trees were also planted next to these altars. Ancient goddess worship was almost always highly sexualized. The priests and priestesses of the goddess were often prostitutes. The worship of the goddess involved having sexual relations with male and female temple prostitutes who represented the goddess and acted as her priests/priestesses.

Fourth century historian Herodotus described the widespread prostitution that took place as part of the worship of the goddess Astarte, known in Babylon as Ishtar. Once in their lifetime, every Babylonian woman was required to sit in the temple of Ishtar and "expose themselves to a stranger" in return for money. In other words, every Babylonian woman was expected to work as a temple prostitute for at least a day. The money she earned was given as an offering in the temple. Everyone needed to participate in the worship of the goddess.

Jezebel was more than just a queen who worshiped Baal and Asherah. Jezebel functioned as a high priestess in Israel, surrounded by the priests and prophets of Baal and Asherah. Four hundred fifty prophets of Baal and four hundred prophets of Asherah ate at her table. In effect, Jezebel ruled over an entire religious system in Israel as the high priestess of the nation.

TOLERANCE

King Ahab came to power in the northern kingdom of Israel while King Asa was king over the southern kingdom of Judah. King Asa did not tolerate idolatry in Judah. But like Jezebel, Asa's grandmother Maachah was a worshiper of Asherah. When Asa came to power (2 Chronicles 14), he removed Maachah from her position as queen mother. He chopped down the idolatrous image of Asherah that Maachah had constructed and burned it at the brook Kidron. He expelled the male and female prostitutes who were part of the religious system of goddess worship in Judah, driving them from the land.

In contrast to King Asa of Judah, King Ahab of Israel was a far more tolerant ruler. The people were free to worship Yahweh as their ancestors had done. They were also free to worship other gods. After all, why should the people of Israel only worship Yahweh? Asherah was worshiped as the wife or consort of the supreme god in Mesopotamian civilizations. Surely Asherah could be worshiped as the feminine counterpart of Yahweh.

Jesus rebuked the church of Thyatira for their tolerance of Jezebel: "You tolerate that woman Jezebel, who calls herself a prophetess" (Revelation 2). The spirit of Jezebel uses the tolerance of God's people to establish her idolatrous systems in their midst.

Likewise, the biblical Queen Jezebel used the tolerance of King Ahab to establish her religious system in Israel. Alongside the worship of Yahweh, the worship of Baal, Asherah, and other gods and goddesses took place. The prostitutes who were such an integral part of goddess worship were welcomed in Israel even as they were rejected in Judah.

In this way, tolerance opened the door for Jezebel to build her religious system. However, Jezebel was not in any way tolerant herself. As soon as she had established her authority, she launched a campaign to eradicate the worship of Yahweh from the land of Israel and to replace it with the worship of Baal and Asherah.

Step by step, Jezebel was able to establish her dominance over the authority structures of Israel. She used her position as queen of Israel to gain control over King Ahab. Once she was able to completely control and manipulate the king, she used his authority to gain control over every governing authority in Israel, including the elders and military force of the nation. She then coerced these governing authorities to persecute her real enemies, the worshipers of Yahweh. The prophets of Yahweh were hunted down by government agents and murdered by the hundreds.

TOTALITARIAN CONTROL

We can get an idea of Jezebel's complete domination over the land of Israel by reading the story of Naboth found in 1 Kings 21:1-24. Naboth owned a vineyard located next to Ahab's palace in Jezreel. Noticing that the vineyard was conveniently located next to his home, Ahab decided it was the perfect place to plant a vegetable garden for himself. Approaching Naboth, he offered to buy his vineyard.

> *So Ahab spoke to Naboth, saying, "Give me your vineyard, that I may have it for a vegetable garden, because it is near, next to my house; and for it I will give you a vineyard better than it. Or, if it seems good to you, I will give you its worth in money." (1 Kings 21:2, NKJV)*

This vineyard had been part of Naboth's family inheritance for many generations since the days of Joshua, so he was unwilling to sell. He responded:

"The LORD forbid that I should give the inheritance of my fathers to you!" (v.3, NKJV).

King Ahab became extremely upset when his offer to buy the vineyard was refused. He retreated to his palace, where he lay on his bed with his face towards the wall, refusing to eat. Approaching the king, Jezebel asked what was troubling him. Ahab informed her that it was because Naboth had refused to sell his vineyard. Jezebel's response demonstrated the power she was wielding in Israel.

> *Then Jezebel his wife said to him, "You now exercise authority over Israel! Arise, eat food, and let your heart be cheerful; I will give you the vineyard of Naboth the Jezreelite." And she wrote letters in Ahab's name, sealed them with his seal, and sent the letters to the elders and the nobles who were dwelling in the city with Naboth. She wrote in the letters, saying, "Proclaim a fast, and seat Naboth with high honor among the people; and seat two men, scoundrels, before him to bear witness against him, saying, 'You have blasphemed God and the king.' Then take him out, and stone him, that he may die. (1 Kings 21:7-10, NKJV)*

Since Jezebel's letters were sealed with the official seal of the king, they carried all the authority of the king. Anyone who refused to obey this direct order would face the full force of the king's retribution. The elders didn't dare to disobey. Proclaiming a fast, they called the people of Naboth's community together and seated Naboth in a position of high honor. At the agreed-upon time, two false witnesses began accusing Naboth of blaspheming God and the king. Naboth was then dragged outside the city and stoned to death.

After completing their assignment, the elders sent a message to Jezebel to inform her that Naboth was dead. Upon receiving the message, Jezebel urged her husband to go take possession of the vineyard, which Ahab promptly did. Meanwhile, God spoke to Elijah the prophet, telling him what had happened and instructing him to confront Ahab for this evil deed.

> *The Lord said to Elijah, "Arise, go down to meet Ahab king of Israel, who lives in Samaria. There he is, in the vineyard of Naboth, where he has gone down to take possession of it. You shall speak to him, saying, 'Thus says the LORD: "Have you murdered and also taken possession?"' And you shall speak to him, saying, 'Thus says the LORD: "In the place where dogs licked the blood of Naboth, dogs shall lick your blood, even yours.""'(1 Kings 21:17-19, NKJV)*

Elijah went to meet King Ahab in Naboth's vineyard. He not only gave Ahab God's message but went on to prophesy God's judgment on Ahab's entire family line and Jezebel as well.

> *"Behold, I [God] will bring calamity on you. I will take away your posterity, and will cut off from Ahab every male in Israel, both bond and free. I will make your house like the house of Jeroboam the son of Nebat, and like the house of Baasha the son of Ahijah, because of the provocation with which you have provoked Me to anger, and made Israel sin." And concerning Jezebel the Lord also spoke, saying, "The dogs shall eat Jezebel by the wall of Jezreel. The dogs shall eat whoever belongs to Ahab and dies in the city, and the birds of the air shall eat whoever dies in the field." (1 Kings 21:21-24, NKJV)*

From this story, we can see the complete dominance Jezebel had gained over Israel. She controlled the king of Israel and issued orders in his name. She controlled the local leaders, the elders of Israel. None dared to stand against her. When she ordered them to condemn an innocent man and stone him to death, they immediately complied.

CHURCH AND STATE

You could say that Jezebel controlled both church and state in Israel. She controlled the state, the governmental system of Israel comprised of the king and other civil authorities. She controlled her own idolatrous religious system, which included the priests and prophets of Asherah and Baal. She combined the authority of church and state together, using the power of the state to force her religion down the throats of the people and using the power of her religion to provide a divine authority, a divine mandate, to the state.

In such a system where the state religion uses the authority of the state to enforce its religious decrees, the state takes upon itself a religious nature. The state takes the place of God in the nation as it combines its authority with the gods of the nation. There is no freedom of religion in such a system. There is no freedom of speech. Anyone who speaks against the state religion will face persecution from government agents. Anyone who speaks against the government is committing a kind of blasphemy because the government is part of the state religion.

This can be seen in the false accusations leveled against Naboth. Naboth's accusers cried out, "Naboth has blasphemed God and the king!" If someone speaking against the king is being accused of blasphemy, then the king has taken the place of God.

This is the system Jezebel had built in Israel, a religious and governmental system that worked to stamp out the true worship of God. In this system, honest men were falsely accused and executed. True prophets of God were murdered. Only the slaves of Jezebel were allowed to remain.

Chapter Two

JEZEBEL'S RELIGIOUS AND GOVERNMENTAL SYSTEM

The biblical Jezebel worked to destroy the existing religious system in Israel even as she worked to replace it with a new system. She also worked to destroy any part of government that resisted her authority even as she worked to build a governmental system completely under her control.

When we speak of a Jezebel spirit and its influence upon America, this spirit works exactly the same way Queen Jezebel worked in Israel. The spirit of Jezebel will try to take control of existing religious and governmental authority. This spirit will try to take control of both the church in a nation and the governmental authority in a nation. This spirit will even try to take control of a nation's economy, schools, and families.

LEGITIMATE GOD-GIVEN AUTHORITY

Jezebel hates and opposes legitimate God-given authority. What is legitimate authority? It is authority that understands the domain it has been given by God. It is authority that understands its limits and works within those limits. It is authority that works for the good of those under its authority.

23

God has ordained authority in every nation, authority that operates with His blessing and purpose. This authority is delegated by God into the hands of fallen humankind. This God-given authority can be found in the family, schools, churches, government, and even in businesses.

Because this authority operates through fallen humankind, it always becomes corrupted to some degree. God gave the rulership of this earth to human beings, and human beings are not holy. Humankind has been deeply corrupted by the evil one as well as by their own lusts and desires. When people exercise their God-given authority over the earth, they do so in a way that is far from God's perfect plan.

Nevertheless, this authority has a legitimate God-given right to operate despite its imperfections. God allows people to use their authority, and to a certain extent He blesses this authority as long as it operates within certain limits. Without this God-given authority, every nation would descend into chaos and anarchy.

For example, a father has legitimate God-given authority in the home. A father is given authority by God to discipline his children in love, protect them, and prepare them for life. A mother's authority is just as important as the authority of a father, although it is somewhat different. A mother nurtures her child. She provides a measure of discipline to the child, but that discipline is not quite the same as a father's discipline.

As a boy, I learned that my mother's threats of punishment were empty. Both my parents engaged in physical discipline, administering spankings and other forms of punishment. But by age ten, I realized my mother was simply not able to physically discipline me in any serious manner. The average woman will find it nearly impossible to administer corporal punishment to a growing teenage boy.

A father protects his home. The right of a father to protect his family is found even in the law of Moses (Exodus 22:2). Under the law of Moses, a father who killed an intruder breaking into his house was not guilty of murder. That father was simply doing his job. It is a man's job to protect his household and family, with force if necessary.

But a father's authority also has limits. A father disciplines his own children, not his neighbor's. A father's discipline lasts for just a few years until his children are ready to start life on their own. When I got married, my father came to me with two scriptures in mind.

"Vaughn, the Bible teaches us to honor our father and mother, that our days may be long (Exodus 20:12). You always need to honor your mother and I as long as you live. The Bible also says 'Children, obey your parents' (Ephesians 6:1). As you get married today, you are no longer a child. You need to honor your mother and me all the days of your life, but you no longer need to obey us. You are now responsible to make your own decisions in life."

My father understood the limits of his authority. He understood that the authority he had to control my choices as a child ended when I became a man.

National governments also have legitimate God-given authority. The first job of a government is to protect its citizens from evil and violent men. A government protects its citizens from criminals within and from the invading armies of enemy nations. God has given the government a tool called the "sword" to protect its citizens. The apostle Paul wrote the following about those who rule in a national government.

> *The authorities are God's servants, sent for your good. But if you are doing wrong, of course you should be afraid, for they have the power to punish you. They are God's servants, sent for the very purpose of punishing those who do what is wrong. (Romans 13:4, NLT)*

A more literal translation says it this way.

> *But if you do what is evil, be afraid; for it does not bear the sword for nothing; for it (governmental authority) is a servant of God, an avenger who brings wrath on the one who practices evil. (Romans 13:4, NASB)*

Human governments are given authority by God to bear the sword and punish evildoers, but they can't change the hearts or thoughts of human beings. They are given the authority to punish evil actions, not evil intentions. The government should never be in the business of punishing thought crimes but only those evil actions that can be proven in a court of law. The sins of the human heart will only be fully revealed on judgment day.

The sword puts fear in the hearts of the thief, murderer, and rapist. The hearts of such people don't really change. They still desire to rape, steal, and murder. But because of the sword in the hands of the government, evil people become afraid to act upon these evil desires. This limits the spread of crime and violence in a nation. When a government uses the sword to punish evil, violent deeds, it is using its God-given authority. When the government focuses on what God has given it to do, it receives grace from God to do its job.

Humanity is fallen, and human governments will always fall short of providing true justice for all. Nevertheless, those governments operate in God-given authority. It is much better for a nation to have an imperfect government than to have no government. When the sword of government is not present, there is nothing to stop rapists, murderers, and thieves from doing what they want to do.

That said, there are many things the sword of government is incapable of doing. The government cannot make everyone equal. The government does not have the right to take the property of one man and give it to another. The government cannot remove racism or other sins of the heart. The government is there to keep law and order so that its citizens can live their lives in peace.

Most importantly, the government is not God and should not try to take the place of God in a nation. It should never force the people to worship a government-sponsored idol or be part of a government sponsored religion. It should not control its people and make them slaves.

Jezebel hates the government that works within its God-given limits, protecting its citizens without compromise. Jezebel tries to gain control of national governments so that the sword of those governments can be used for illegitimate purposes. She tries to use government to persecute those who resist her and to coerce people into the worship of her idols.

The spirit of Jezebel is ultimately a spirit of control working to control everyone and everything. She works ceaselessly to usurp authority that has not been given to her by God. She typically works in a hidden way behind the scenes to infiltrate and manipulate every form of authority in a nation. When authorities refuse to surrender control to Jezebel, she works to undermine them, discredit them, and ultimately destroy them.

SYSTEMS OF DARKNESS

In my book *Open Heavens: A Biblical Guide to High-Level Spiritual Warfare*, I teach about the way in which the "god of this world" (2 Corinthians 4:4), the devil himself, rules over the earth. To a large degree, the devil uses religious and governmental systems to rule over humankind.

One example of these systems is Islam, which is both a religious and governmental system that rules over 1.4 billion of the earth's inhabitants. Another example of a system used by the evil one to rule this earth is Communism. In a communist system such as the former USSR, North Korea, and China, the government completely controls the people, religion, and economy of the nation. The communist party forms a kind of religion, outlawing and displacing other religions.

These systems combine religion and government so that church and state act as one. Because government takes the place of God, speaking against the official "religion" of the system is considered blasphemy and will result in persecution from government authorities just as occurred to Naboth.

FIVE ELEMENTS OF A SYSTEM

Every system used by the evil one has five main elements:

- An idol
- A priesthood
- Covenants
- Evil spiritual rulers
- Lies

At the center of each evil system is the idol, something that takes the place of God. In a communist nation, the communist party and perhaps the supreme leader becomes the idol. In an Islamic nation, the "perfect" man Mohammed and his book the Koran take the place of God. Muslims believe the Koran existed in heaven before the world was created.

Every system also has a priesthood. The priests enforce the worship of the idol. They teach the people exactly how the idol must be worshiped. The priesthood in a communist nation is made up of the government officials who ensure that nobody ever speaks against their idol, the communist party. If you speak out against the party, the priests of communism may have you killed or banished to a slave-labor camp. In Islam, the priests are the religious leaders, imams, and mullahs. If you speak a word against Mohammed or his book, they will condemn you to death.

Each system controlled by darkness also has evil spiritual rulers. These rulers are the "rulers of the darkness of this age" the apostle Paul taught about, the principalities and powers, fallen angels, invisible spiritual armies working in union with the devil to rule over this world (Ephesians 6:12, NKJV).

Every system also has covenants that connect the humans in the system to the evil spiritual rulers. A covenant binds two people together. The strongest form of covenant is a blood covenant. A blood covenant costs a person's life.

The first description in the Bible of a blood covenant is actually found in the story of Adam and Eve. Jesus spoke of this union that took place when Adam and Eve were created.

A man will leave his father and mother, and be united to his wife, and two will become one flesh. (Matthew 19:5, NIV)

In the blood covenant of marriage, two become one. A woman's body is created in such a way that when she has sexual intercourse for the first time, there is blood. This demonstrates that the covenant formed between a man and a woman is a blood covenant, costing the life of the covenant partners. In this covenant, the husband gives up his life for the sake of his wife and family. He no longer lives and works for himself but for his covenant partner. Likewise, a woman gives her life for her husband and her children, loving and serving them.

There are two main ways in which blood covenants are formed. Sexual intercourse is a kind of blood covenant, joining two people together. Blood sacrifices are also used to form blood covenants. The devil uses both of these forms of covenant to join human beings to himself and his evil spiritual rulers. Throughout the Bible, we read about blood sacrifices offered to idols. Baal and other evil spiritual beings were worshiped with blood sacrifices. Animals would be sacrificed to Baal, then the worshipers would eat the roasted meat of those sacrifices. As they ate the meat, they formed a blood covenant between themselves and Baal. He became their god, and they became his people.

Likewise, we repeatedly read about temple prostitutes in the Bible. Worshipers of Baal and other deities would go to their temples to have sexual relations with prostitutes dedicated to those false gods. As the worshipers engaged in sexual intercourse with these prostitutes, they formed blood covenants between themselves and the gods for whom these prostitutes worked. In this way, men and women connected themselves to Baal, Asherah, and other evil deities.

These covenants can be found in every religious and governmental system in one form or another. In Islam, for example, once a year every Muslim is expected to sacrifice a sheep in the "Festival of the Sacrifice" (Eid a-Adha). Likewise, every Muslim is expected to make a pilgrimage (Hajj) to visit Mecca in Saudi Arabia once in his lifetime. On the third day of the Hajj, every pilgrim must sacrifice an animal or buy a voucher paying for the sacrifice of an animal on his behalf. These blood sacrifices connect every Muslim to the evil spiritual forces that rule over the Islamic religion.

Finally, every one of these false systems contains lies. The central lie in each system involves the nature of God. The idol of the system is said to be God. The nature of this idol causes a twisted view of righteousness, of what is good and what is evil.

For example, in the system of Islam, everything Mohammed did is considered to be righteous. Mohammed lied, stole, murdered, and raped his captives. Every time he did something evil, he received a revelation from his "angel" saying that Allah was the one leading him to do these evil deeds. In this way, lies about the nature of good and evil are implanted in the very center of the Islamic system. If Mohammed is the light of your life, the one leading you to righteousness, the one showing you the difference between good and evil, many abominations will be called good and many good things will be condemned as evil. Jesus Himself testified to this sad truth.

> *If the light that is in you is darkness, how great is that darkness!*
> *(Matthew 6:23. NIV)*

These five elements of an evil system are described in greater detail with further examples in my book *Open Heavens: A Biblical Guide to High-Level Spiritual Warfare.*

JEZEBEL THE SYSTEM BUILDER

Jezebel is the system builder. In the land of Israel, she built a religious and governmental system centered around the worship of Baal and Asherah. This system had its central idols, priesthood, evil spiritual rulers, blood covenants, and lies like every other system controlled by darkness. Baal and Asherah were the idols in the center of the system. Jezebel raised up a priesthood consisting of four hundred fifty prophets of Baal and four hundred prophets of Asherah that enforced the worship of Baal and Asherah.

But Baal and Asherah were more than mere wooden idols. Behind the idols were evil spiritual beings, rulers of darkness working in league with the devil. These evil rulers were the real power behind the system. Jezebel led the nation in the worship of these false gods. The nation of Israel bowed before Baal and kissed his idol. The nation of Israel worshiped these gods with blood sacrifices. They participated in sexual perversion with prostitutes dedicated to these false gods.

The blood sacrifices and sexual perversion formed blood covenants between the people of Israel and Baal and Asherah. The children of Israel became the children of Baal, connected to him in covenant. He became their god, and they became his people. The children of Israel broke their covenant with the God of Abraham, Isaac, and Jacob and formed an adulterous relationship with Baal and Asherah.

And of course, this system was full of lies. We read about the lies and accusations leveled against Naboth. We read that it was considered blasphemy to speak against the king. Good was called evil, and evil was called good. Righteous men were murdered while cowards and accusers rose into positions of power. Elijah, the prophet who loved and served God, was called the "troubler of Israel" (1 Kings 18:17) by King Ahab, the one who truly brought trouble to Israel.

Chapter Three

JEZEBEL'S NEW RELIGIOUS SYSTEM

Jezebel's ultimate goal is not just to control a nation. Jezebel is a globalist. She desires to build a system that will control the entire world. She can actually be compared to the Whore of Babylon described in Revelation 17-18. This woman "sits on many waters" (v. 1), representing "multitudes, nations, and tongues" (v. 15). She fornicates with the kings of the earth (v. 2). She controls and manipulates these earthly rulers. She "reigns over the kings of the earth" (v. 18). She uses sorcery to deceive the nations (18:23). She is called Babylon, the great city that reigns over the kings of the earth.

This Babylon represents all the religious, governmental, and economic systems that are used by the evil one to keep the earth in spiritual darkness. There are many religious and governmental systems of differing size and influence in this world, yet all are a part of this greater system, the system of Babylon. In the last days, this Babylonian world system will attempt to completely dominate the nations of the world just as Queen Jezebel dominated Israel.

In her quest for world domination, there is one nation with more power and influence than any other, the United States of America. If Jezebel hopes to dominate this world, she must gain control of this nation. For this reason, Jezebel focuses her attacks on this nation more than any other.

The religious, governmental, and economic system Jezebel is attempting to build in America today has many similarities to the system Queen Jezebel built in Israel. If America is able to resist Jezebel's plans, other nations will also be freed from her grasp. If Jezebel is able to finish the construction of her system in America, much of the world will be brought into bondage.

Jezebel's system in America will be built around the worship of an idol, something or someone that takes the place of God. It will have a priesthood, those who are extreme in their loyalty to the idol and who enforce its worship. Pulling the strings behind this system are evil spiritual rulers connected to the American people through blood covenants. This system will be built upon lies and will produce a river of lies that flows through all of American society.

AMERICAN IDOL

To understand the system the spirit of Jezebel is building in America today, we must first look at the idol she is building it around, something or someone that takes the place of God. In Israel, Jezebel built her system around the worship of Baal and Asherah, the false gods of Mesopotamia. But who is the false god of America?

The false gods of our society are not as obvious as the gods of Phoenicia. In America today, we do not have temples built to worship Baal and Asherah. We do not serve evil deities that speak through human priests and prophets, demanding human sacrifices. We do not typically eat meat sacrificed to idols. America's prostitutes are not priestesses who openly seduce men in the name of their goddess.

Nevertheless, there is a false god taking the place of God in America, and Jezebel is building her religious and governmental system around that idol. Some would say money is America's false god, the idol living in the hearts of the people. Money can surely become an idol. Jesus warned his followers about the idol of money.

> *No one can serve two masters. Either you will hate the one and love the other, or you will be devoted to the one and despise the other. You cannot serve both God and money. (Matthew 6:24, NIV)*

While certainly an idol in America, is money really the central idol? Do we teach our children to believe in money and worship money? Or is there another idol more central to Jezebel's system in America than money? Yes! If you took the time to watch children's movies coming out of Hollywood, what is the underlying message repeated time and time again? Believe in yourself!

Likewise in our public schools, children are not taught to believe in God. They are taught to believe in themselves. They are not taught to love God or money. They are taught to love themselves. They are taught that the most noble, good thing someone can do is to believe in oneself, be true to oneself, and love oneself. Self is the central idol in the system Jezebel is building in America.

LUSTS OF THE FLESH

When the idol of self takes the place of God, the lusts of the flesh become sacred. If you are your own god, then the desires of your heart and lusts of your flesh become sacred because they come from your god.

This can be seen in the exaltation of sexual lust that takes place in our nation. Perverse sexual desires are celebrated in our nation. In most societies, it is considered a noble thing to serve one's deity or serve one's country. In our society, it is considered a noble thing to obey one's sexual desire. If a man needs to leave his wife and his children to have a sexual relationship with another man, it is a noble and good thing. He is obeying his desire. He is being true to himself, true to his god.

Sexual desire and lust of the flesh must therefore be a good thing, even a sacred thing, because it comes from self. It is no longer acceptable in American society to say that homosexual lust and sexual activity are sinful. It is becoming illegal in America to counsel a homosexual and lead them to repentance for their sexual activities. Many would now consider such counsel to be a kind of hate crime.

When self is god, there cannot be a higher God who proclaims that the desires of self are wrong. God determines what is good and evil, what is right and wrong. When self is god, human beings decide what is good and what is evil without any need for moral guidance from a higher God. Whatever we decide is good is good. Whatever we decide is evil is evil.

Our Creator is no longer permitted to decide if we are male or female. We decide if we are male or female. When a young girl decides that she is actually a boy, she magically becomes a boy. It is now becoming illegal in America to counsel that young girl that she is actually a girl with the body of a girl. Many would consider it a kind of hate crime to tell that young girl she is not a boy. School officials and mental health professionals all quickly fall in line to support the young girl's profession that she is a boy.

The man who declares that only men have penises is guilty of hate speech and can easily lose his job. The woman who declares that only women can give birth is guilty of hate speech and can easily lose her job. Those who make such views public on YouTube or Instagram are finding that they are being blocked from these platforms by administrators who believe that such views are hateful and beyond the scope of acceptable political discourse.

The federal government has issued its mandates that all schools must treat transgender students according to their preferred gender. The young man who insists he is a female must be allowed access to the girl's locker rooms and vice versa.

HUMANISM

The philosophy that accompanies the exaltation of self and selfish desire in America is the philosophy of secular humanism. Secular humanism is a philosophy that elevates human reason, human ethics, and a materialistic world view while rejecting both God and religion as a source for morality and decision-making. Secular humanists generally believe there is no God or that if God exists, His existence has little to do with human affairs. Human reason alone can determine what is good and provide a moral and ethical foundation for society.

The forces of secular humanism cloak themselves in reason and science. They claim to offer a realistic, unbiased view of reality. Those who have developed a strong distaste for religion delude themselves that they are trading foolishness and superstition for the cold, hard truth of science.

Humanist scientists can look at the mind-blowing complexity of life with designs infinitely beyond anything found in computers. They can study the very blueprints of creation, the genetic code through which all the incredible manifestations of life have been designed. Yet even in the face of such overwhelming complexity, they still believe that nothing created everything and that all arose through blind chance.

In secular humanism, a person's own mind becomes the idol at the center of the system. This is spiritual blindness on a scale that outweighs the blindness of the most deluded religious leaders. It is foolishness and arrogance on a scale that is almost incomprehensible. Nevertheless, it is the reality of western civilization where so many have become incapable of recognizing a Creator greater than themselves but instead exalt themselves above God and despise even the mention of God.

Humanists don't believe their lives and deeds will ever be judged by a righteous God. On the contrary, humanists presume to judge God, attacking God's actions as immoral and searching the Bible for what they believe to be evidence of God's misogynism, barbarity, racism, and terrorism. This is the work of Jezebel and the idolatry of self.

AMERICAN CHRISTIANITY

American religious observance has undergone a rapid decline due to the effects of humanism. Nearly half of Americans attend church once a year or less. Only twenty-two percent of Americans attend church on a weekly basis. Nevertheless, most Americans still claim to believe in God, and most Americans still claim to be Christian.

But what God do we believe in? The God many Americans believe in accepts us just as we are without repentance or change. He accepts our sexual sin and helps us to love and accept ourselves just the way we are. He supports every choice we make. He affirms us and comforts us no matter what we do. America's "god" always supports and affirms the higher god, the god of self.

Self-fulfillment is the realizing of one's deepest desires and capacities. Many American Christians believe that a good church will help one's quest for self-fulfillment. Church is not a place where one learns to crucify his desires and ambitions so that the desires of God can fill his heart. Church is a place where one obtains God's help in fulfilling his own desires and ambitions.

Many American "Christians" don't really believe in sin. Generally speaking, many Americans believe in sickness, not in sin. They believe in victims, not sinners. A drunkard is not a sinner. He is a victim of the sickness of alcoholism. The promiscuous woman is not a sinner. She is the victim of a string of bad relationships, or perhaps she suffers from the sickness of sexual addiction. Even our criminals are not really sinners. The murderer is the victim of an abusive childhood. The person who breaks into our house grew up in an underprivileged environment. And so forth.

Our morality is not determined by what the Word of God says. Our morality is determined by what makes people feel good. We never want someone to feel condemned or that what they did is wrong.

Many American Christians believe that Jesus never judged anybody and that His central message was to love and accept everyone. They don't believe God ever condemns anyone to hell except possibly Adolf Hitler and similar monsters. They believe in a broad road leading to salvation. That everything will work out well in the end. That most of us have nothing to fear when we face eternity.

They ignore the fact that Jesus spoke a more terrifying message of judgment than anyone else in the Bible. Jesus taught of a narrow road leading to salvation that is found by only a few (Matthew 7:13-14). He taught repeatedly of the fires and horror of hell (Matthew 8:12; 13:24-50; 22:1-14; 24:51; 25:14-46; Mark 9:43; Luke 13:28). If you believe the words of Jesus, you will also believe in the judgments of God.

Many American Christians question the exclusivity of Christianity. There are many good religions, they will say, many paths to God. Christians should be tolerant of other religions. There are good people who know God in every religion. Who is to say that we are better than anyone else?

Jezebel will always reveal a god of tolerance, a god who accepts humankind's evil covenants of false religion and sexual immorality. This false god accepts us without trying to change us. He supports every decision we make and everything we want to do.

This is the sad reality of America today. The idol of self is taking the place of the true God in our schools, churches, government, and families. Jezebel is building a religious and governmental system around this idol just as she did in Israel.

BLOOD COVENANTS

Covenants are very important in every system Jezebel builds. Covenants connect the people who are under the system with the evil spiritual rulers who control the system. Covenants connect Americans to the devil and his rulers of darkness, including Jezebel herself. And just as in the days of Queen Jezebel, these covenants take two main forms—sexual immorality and blood sacrifices.

The spread of technology has enabled lust, sexual perversion, and immorality to spread through American society at an unprecedented rate. When I was a child in the 1970s, Playboy magazines with their photos of nude women sat high on magazine shelves, hidden behind special covers. A man really needed to go out of his way to obtain pornography. And the pornography available in those days almost seems innocent compared to what is available today.

Today pornography floods the internet, overwhelming its viewers with its incredible quantity and variety of sexual acts. Every sick and twisted sexual fantasy that has ever invaded human minds is only a click away. A large percentage of American men have literally become enslaved to pornography. They are no longer turned on by Playboy centerfolds but feel compelled to seek out scenes of the most deviant sexual behavior. Many try to act out their fantasies in real life, connecting with men and women on Tinder and other "dating" apps that provide easy, commitment-free sexual connections to satisfy one's lust.

Sexual immorality and pornography are controlled by the spirit of Jezebel, who uses them to form covenants between humankind and unclean spirits. When human beings obey spirits of lust and perversion, they become the slaves of Jezebel and part of the system she is building.

BLOOD SACRIFICES

Since the supreme god of America is the god of self, Jezebel works to ensure that this false god receives blood sacrifices. In ancient times, the Phoenicians became notorious for the thousands of child sacrifices they offered to their gods. In modern times, the spirit of Jezebel is the spirit behind child sacrifices offered to the false god of self in America.

When people behave selfishly and exalt every lust and desire, there are always unwelcome consequences such as pregnancy. If having a baby interferes with a woman's education or career or her male sexual partner views a baby as an obstacle to his plans and ambitions, too often that baby is offered up as a blood offering to the god of self. In the United States alone, more than fifty million abortions have taken place since 1973 when the Supreme Court legalized abortion in the infamous court ruling Roe vs. Wade.

When a woman aborts her baby, she is declaring that her own self-interest, her own idea of success in life, is more valuable than the life of her child. She is declaring that her god of self is worthy to be worshiped with the blood of her child.

The servants of Jezebel are extreme in their commitment to abortion rights. They resist any and all restrictions on abortion. They work to ensure that American women are able to have abortions even in their ninth month of pregnancy and beyond.

Some of America's most influential politicians have even displayed a commitment to the brutal practice of partial birth abortion. In a partial birth abortion, the abortionist grabs the feet of the baby with his forceps to deliver it feet first. The entire body is pulled out of the birth canal with only the baby's head remaining inside the mother. The abortionist then jams his scissors into the baby's skull's and inserts a suction catheter to suck out the baby's brains, collapsing its skull. The lifeless body is then completely removed from its mother and discarded.

It would seem common human decency would cause such a brutal practice to be condemned. Yet Bill Clinton vetoed a law in 1996 that would have outlawed partial birth abortion. Hillary Clinton, Barack Obama, and Joe Biden have all supported a woman's right to have partial birth abortions.

Sometimes babies survive the attempts of the abortionist to kill them. In 2003, the Illinois state legislature passed the Born Alive Infant Protection Act that recognized babies surviving abortions as being persons entitled to medical care. A federal "born-alive" bill was also passed by Congress in 2002 without a single opposing vote. Not even NARAL, the extreme abortion rights activist group, opposed it. Yet Barack Obama voted against this act three times, demonstrating a commitment to abortion and even infanticide that went beyond even the most extreme abortion activists.

Why are some of our most influential politicians so extreme in their support of abortion rights? These politicians are part of the evil system Jezebel is building.

They are not fighting for the rights of women. They are literally fighting for the blood sacrifices themselves, sacrifices that empower the religious system built around the idol of self.

As these sacrifices are offered, humans become bound by blood covenant to the god of self. In a blood covenant, two become one. The people of America give themselves completely to their idol while offering up their own children as sacrifices.

EVERYONE NEEDS TO PARTICIPATE

One of the main goals of Obamacare was to force people to buy health insurance the government required them to purchase instead of the health care plans people actually wanted to purchase. When the government forces everyone to buy certain health care plans, it can also stipulate what is covered by those plans.

The Obama administration tried to use Obamacare to force a group of Catholic nuns known as the Little Sisters to provide contraception that included "morning after pills" and other abortifacients to their employees. The nuns were threatened with millions of dollars in fines when they refused to submit to this government coercion. The nuns took the case all the way to the Supreme court as they fought for their religious liberty. The court ruled in their favor, and the sisters won at least a temporary victory.

Of course, the real goal of these servants of Jezebel is not to force people to purchase contraception but to force religious groups to go against their conscience and pay for abortion. It is very important to the servants of Jezebel that every person in America be required to purchase health care that includes coverage of abortion.

In 2019, the Trump administration required that every Obamacare plan collect payment for abortion coverage separately from other health care insurance payments. This rule made it easy for those who didn't want to pay for abortion coverage in their health care plan not to pay it. At the present time, the Biden administration is proposing to eliminate this rule so that insurance companies can hide abortion coverage in their plans. The next step is very predictable. As Jezebel increases her grip on this nation, you can be sure that every health care plan in America will soon be required to include coverage for abortion.

Universal forced worship of the idol is one of the signs of Jezebel. During the reign of Nebuchadnezzar, every citizen of Babylon was required to bow down to the golden idol of himself that Nebuchadnezzar had created (Daniel 3). According to Herodotus, every Babylonian woman was required to participate in temple prostitution at least once in her life. Every Muslim is required to offer animal sacrifices in Islamic rituals.

Similarly, it is very important to the servants of Jezebel that every American citizen be compelled to pay for abortion and celebrate gay marriage and sexual perversion. In this way, everyone takes part in worshipping the god of self, and everyone is connected by blood covenant to the idol and spiritual beings represented by the idol. The control of Jezebel's system is extended into every home.

This is the system Jezebel is building in America. When this system is fully formed, it will be illegal to speak against the idol and illegal to speak against the government. Freedom of speech and freedom of religion will be outlawed. Everyone will be forced to participate in the new religion and take part in its rituals.

We are not far from the complete implementation of this system. The spirit of Jezebel is systematically attacking and removing every form of authority that opposes her complete control of our land. The idol is in place. The covenants have been formed between the people and the evil spiritual rulers who rule over the system. A priesthood protects the idol of self and viciously attacks anyone who refuses to submit to Jezebel. We will talk more about these priests in chapter ten.

And of course, this system is full of lies, which we will discuss in much more detail in following chapters. Good is called evil, and evil is called good. The Bible itself is condemned, the God of the Bible is condemned, and those who believe in both of them are condemned as intolerant, ignorant, and hateful. They are no longer allowed to be a central part of American society but are systematically being pushed to the fringes. Soon they will be outlawed, and Jezebel's reign of terror will begin.

Chapter Four

THE AMERICAN SYSTEM OF LIMITED CONSTITUTIONAL GOVERNMENT

J ezebel works to build a religious and governmental system in which church and state are closely entwined. A system in which the state religion is empowered by the government. A system in which the government takes the place of God in the nation.

As Jezebel works to build her worldwide religious and governmental system, she faces many obstacles. One of the biggest obstacles to Jezebel's control within the United States is the American constitution. The United States of America is a constitutional republic in which the Constitution of the United States is the supreme law of the land. This constitution restricts the authority and actions of the United States government, providing a system of limited constitutional government. An understanding of the American system of limited government can be found by studying the preamble to the Declaration of Independence.

> *We hold these truths to be self-evident, that all men are created equal, that they are endowed by their Creator with certain unalienable Rights, that among these are Life, Liberty and the pursuit of Happiness. That to secure these rights, Governments are instituted among Men, deriving*

their just powers from the consent of the governed. That whenever any Form of Government becomes destructive of these ends, it is the Right of the People to alter or to abolish it, and to institute new Government, laying its foundation on such principles and organizing its powers in such form, as to them shall seem most likely to effect their Safety and Happiness.

In the American system, it is understood that people are given unalienable rights by their Creator. These rights include life, liberty, and the pursuit of happiness. The purpose of government is to protect these God-given rights of the people. If there is no government, then violent and greedy men can trample on our rights. Without government, foreign nations can invade and enslave the people. Without government, violent gangs can take control of neighborhoods, trampling on the rights of the people.

According to the Declaration of Independence, governments are not given their authority by God but from the consent of the governed. The people receive their rights from God, but government receives its authority from the people. This means government is not divine. If the government does not perform its primary duty of protecting the rights of the people, the people have the right and responsibility to overthrow that government and institute a new government.

This original American understanding of government places very strict limits upon governments. The government is not allowed to take the place of God. While the people are free, the government is not free but operates under strict limits.

In 1787, the founding fathers of America formed a constitution that clearly set forth the role of government and limits of governmental authority. In Section 8 of Article One of the Constitution, the government is given a very limited list of responsibilities, or "enumerated powers." These enumerated powers include the power to tax, to spend, borrow, and coin money to regulate commerce between the states and with foreign nations, to establish post offices and roads, to regulate patents and copyrights, to establish courts, to raise up and support a military, and to declare war.

The duties of the United States government as described in the constitution are quite different from the constitutions of many other nations. The duties of the American government do not include a mandate to provide health care for all of America's citizens. The constitution does not include a mandate to provide education for every American. It does not promise to provide jobs and retirement income for all Americans.

Quite simply, a government that promises jobs for all must be able to completely control that nation's economy and businesses owned by private citizens. The government that promises health care for all needs to completely control the nation's health care system. The government that promises education for all needs to completely control the educational system. The more a government promises to do for its people, the more the people come under the suffocating control of government. This was not the role the founding fathers envisioned for the United States government.

GOVERNMENTAL RESTRICTIONS

The American constitution is not a compilation of government promises committing the government to care for Americans from cradle to grave. Rather, the constitution contains an extensive list of things the government is not permitted to do. The first amendment of the constitution reads as follows.

> *Congress shall make no law respecting an establishment of religion, or prohibiting the free exercise thereof; or abridging the freedom of speech, or of the press; or the right of the people peaceably to assemble, and to petition the Government for a redress of grievances.*

In other words, the government of the United States is not permitted to take away the right of the people to protest against government actions (, i.e., "petition the government for the redress of grievances"). The government of the United States is not allowed to take away the people's right to assemble and hold meetings. It is not allowed to take away their freedom of speech or freedom of press.

More importantly, the government is not allowed to take away the people's freedom of religion. It is not permitted to establish an official "state" religion. It is not allowed to stop people from freely exercising the religion of their choice or prohibit people of a disfavored religion from holding positions in government. Article 6 of the constitution reads:

> *No religious Test shall ever be required as a Qualification to any Office or public Trust under the United States.*

The right to property is also protected in the Constitution. The government is not allowed to just take people's property without due process of law. The Fifth Amendment states:

> *No person shall be deprived of life, liberty, or property, without due process of law; nor shall private property be taken for public use, without just compensation.*

Neither is government allowed to confiscate people's property through imposing excessive fines. The Eighth Amendment speaks to this as well as fair treatment within the judicial and law enforcement systems.

> *Excessive bail shall not be required, nor excessive fines imposed, nor cruel and unusual punishments inflicted.*

The Constitution also recognizes the God-given right of the people to protect themselves. The Second Amendment states:

A well regulated Militia, being necessary to the security of a free State, the right of the people to keep and bear Arms, shall not be infringed.

The mention of a "militia" and "the security of a free State" makes clear the Second Amendment was not added to just to protect the right to shoot squirrels or other game but the right of citizens to protect themselves, from their own government if necessary. If the government should ever become tyrannical, trampling the rights of the people instead of protecting those rights, the people have the right to protect themselves from their own government. The end result is a government that is severely limited and a people that are free. This is the American system of government.

Which isn't to say our constitutional system of government is or was perfect. From the beginning of our nation, deep compromises were made regarding issues of freedom. The same founding fathers who took a stand against Great Britain when they believed their freedoms were being infringed upon refused to take a stand against slavery. Even the founding fathers who opposed slavery believed they needed the support of slave-owning colonies to win their fight against Great Britain.

In consequence, protections for the "rights" of slaveowners were embedded in the American constitution. These protections included the "fugitive slave clause" that guaranteed slaves who escaped and sought refuge in northern states would be returned to their masters. These compromises were only removed at great cost during the Civil War, which took place more than seventy years after the Constitution of the United States was ratified.

In spite of these deep flaws, the Constitution of the United States helped produce a nation which the evil one was never able to completely control. The devil was never able to build a religious and governmental system in the United States like he did in Islamic and Communist nations because the constitution limited the role of government and kept it from taking the place of God.

Today, there are many people who want to condemn the American constitution and remove its limitations on the federal government. They claim that the reasons they want to remove the constitution is because of its flaws, because the founding fathers were racists and slave owners. In reality, the enemies of our constitution want to remove its authority because of the things the constitution got right, not because of the things it got wrong. They don't actually hate the constitution because some of the founders were slave owners. They hate it because it restricts what they want to do with the federal government.

America's constitutional government helped it become known as the land of the free, a place where people were free to worship God as they chose. It is known as a land where people can say what they want about their government without fear of reprisal. A place where people are protected from the tyrannical depredations of government. A place where elections are thought to be free and fair. A nation ruled by a government of the people, by the people, and for the people. It became a nation that stood for economic freedom, a place where anyone could work hard and prosper without needing to fear the fruits of their labor would be taken from them by force.

As long as the United States of America adheres to its own constitution, a state religion cannot be imposed upon the people. As long as the United States adheres to its own constitution, Jezebel cannot build her religious and governmental system over the nation.

ENSLAVING THE PEOPLE

The Jezebel spirit is ultimately a control spirit, the enemy of true freedom. In the system Jezebel is building, the rights of the people that are protected in the constitution will be done away with. In the new system, the government will trample on property rights just as Jezebel stole the property of Naboth.

 In the new system, nobody will have the right of free speech. If you speak against the government in Jezebel's system, you will be condemned just as Naboth was condemned. You will be accused of committing blasphemy against God and the king, blasphemy against the government that takes the place of God in the nation.

In the new system, there will be no right of assembly. When people gather together in large groups, they might start planning a rebellion against the government. In the new system, people will only be allowed to gather in very small groups. It is dangerous to allow people to assemble freely.

In the new system, the people will no longer be allowed to engage in protests against their government. Jezebel does not tolerate dissension. Those who protest against government actions will be dealt with swiftly and brutally.

And of course, there will be no freedom of religion in Jezebel's system. In Jezebel's system, everybody will bow down to the idol of self. Nobody will be permitted to speak against sexual perversion or Jezebel's state-sponsored idolatry. Churches will not be permitted to teach about sexual morality from a biblical standpoint. They will not be permitted to operate their own schools in which children are taught biblical morality.

Jezebel will systematically tear down every authority that is capable of resisting her. Parents will lose all authority to train their children and discipline their children in the ways of the Lord. Children will be taught the religion of self by state-appointed teachers. They will be taught that good is evil and evil is good. Their teachers will lead them in religious rituals by which idolatrous covenants are formed.

It goes without saying that the people will not be permitted to keep and bear arms. An armed people is a people that is difficult to control. Every totalitarian system must remove weapons from the hands of the people lest the people think they can resist the total control of the government.

In fact, every right and freedom presently protected by our constitutional system of government will be systematically done away with if Jezebel has her way. Jezebel's disciples will not be satisfied until every constitutional limitation of the authority of government is removed. Jezebel needs a totalitarian government at the center of her system, a government that will enforce and empower her religion.

THE MOST SACRED CONSTITUTIONAL RIGHT

Although the servants of Jezebel want to do away with the right to bear arms, economic freedom, the freedom of religion, speech, press, assembly, and protest, there is one constitutional right they do want to protect. A right the servants of Jezebel believe is more important than any other. A right to which they give their unwavering support. This is the right of a woman to have an abortion.

The servants of Jezebel believe that a woman's right to have an abortion is a fundamental human right protected by our constitution. That the constitution says nothing at all about abortion means nothing to them. That our constitution is intrinsically connected to the Declaration of Independence, which recognizes a God-given right to life, means nothing to them. That "sex-selective" abortions are used around the world to end the lives of far more female babies than male babies means nothing to these supporters of "women's rights."

The only thing that matters to these abortion zealots is that in 1972 the Supreme Court of the United States invented a right to abortion and declared that all restrictions on abortion are unconstitutional. The supporters of abortion think that the 1972 case of Roe vs Wade is a "super precedent," a Supreme court ruling that must be honored and obeyed for all eternity despite the fact that this ruling was clearly unconstitutional.

In this way, rights and freedoms clearly protected by the American constitution are done away with while a right that was never in our constitution is enshrined as the supreme law of our land. This is the work of Jezebel, a sign that her attempt to transform the American system of government is succeeding.

As stated in the previous chapter, Jezebel's support for abortion has nothing to do with women's rights. Jezebel doesn't actually care about women's rights any more than she does about anyone else's rights. She desires to make all of us slaves of her new system. Abortion is important to her because it is the glue that holds her entire system together. It is the blood sacrifice that connects the people to the idol of self and to the evil spiritual rulers who empower her entire system.

Chapter Five

THE METHODS OF JEZEBEL

If we hope to thwart Jezebel's takeover of our nation, we must understand the way Jezebel works. Jezebel's ultimate goal is clear. Her ultimate plan is to build a controlling religious, economic, and governmental system over our nation.

To accomplish this ultimate plan, Jezebel has three basic goals. First of all, Jezebel works to gain control over every form of authority that resists her purposes. She works to hijack legitimate authority, to use its power for her illegitimate purposes. If those in legitimate authority resist her attempts to control and manipulate them, Jezebel works to have them destroyed.

Secondly, Jezebel works to convince people to "commit sexual immorality and eat things sacrificed to idols" (Revelation 2:20). In other words, she works to bind people in evil covenants through engaging them in different forms of idolatry and sexual immorality.

Thirdly, Jezebel builds a network of lies. These lies have to do with the nature of God, the nature of good and evil. She lies about the idol of self, teaching people that the lusts of the flesh are good. She lies about the nature of God as she condemns the God of the Bible.

Nearly everything Jezebel does is for the purpose of achieving these three goals—to tear down or gain control over legitimate authority, to bring people into evil covenants, and to spread lies about the nature of God and of good and evil.

THE TEACHINGS OF JEZEBEL

But how does Jezebel accomplish these goals? What are her methods? The words of Jesus through the apostle John to the church at Thyatira lays out her methods clearly.

> *You allow that woman Jezebel, who calls herself a prophetess, to teach and seduce My servants to commit sexual immorality and eat things sacrificed to idols. (Revelation 2:20, NKJV)*

Jezebel calls herself a prophetess. Jezebel teaches and seduces God's people. In other words, she is using the three-fold method of teaching, seduction, and prophecy to accomplish her three main goals. In this chapter, we will take a closer look at the teaching, seduction, and prophecy of Jezebel.

So what does Jezebel teach, and how can we recognize her teachings? In truth, Jezebel's teachings can easily be recognized if you look past the arguments being presented to the goal of the teaching because Jezebel has very discernable goals. First, her teachings will always work to delegitimatize and undermine people's trust in legitimate authority.

Targets of Jezebel's teaching will include the American constitutional system of limited government. Jezebel needs a much more controlling form of government to accomplish her purposes, so she will systematically teach in a way that destroys the American people's confidence in their own constitutional system. When Jezebel teaches about American history, for instance, the history lessons will consist of a long list of the faults and failures of the American system.

For example, the 1619 Project is a school curriculum project sponsored by the New York Times that attempts to retell the American story. In 1619, the first slaves were shipped to the American colonies. According to the 1619 Project, this is the beginning of the American story. The Revolutionary War was fought to protect slavery. America was founded to protect slavery. The story of America is a story primarily about slavery.

There is no sense of balance in this teaching, no discussion of the various forms of slavery and extreme oppression that have existed in every society throughout human history. There is no emphasis on the positive aspects of American history, just a laser-like focus on the worst parts so that all of American history can be condemned.

Students who study history in this way become convinced that America is uniquely evil among the nations of the world. They become very open to the idea that our history is so evil and oppressive we should literally start over. Our constitutional system of limited government should be abolished and a new, more equitable system should be established.

Jezebel's teachings also seek to bring about the blood covenants of sexual immorality and the eating of "things sacrificed to idols." When Jezebel gains entrance into a Christian institution such as a school or a church, she immediately begins working to spread her teachings about these covenants. She does this by teaching Christians that other religions are just different ways of approaching the same God. She teaches that there are many paths to God and that all will be saved. She teaches about the good things found in all religions and encourages Christians to participate in the religious rituals of other religions. She works to bring elements of Islam, Buddhism, Hinduism, and Native American spirituality into the church.

Human religions are idolatrous. If there was an easier way to reconcile humanity to a holy God, would God have sent His Son to die on a cross? Salvation is found in no one else for there is no other name under heaven given to humankind by which we must be saved (Acts 4:12). It is only by the name of Jesus. He is the only way to the Father (John 14:6).

This is the offense of the cross, the offense of Christianity. The religions of humankind offer substitute gods and substitute paths to God that blind people's eyes and deaden their hearts so that they do not see the horror of their lost condition. These false religions seem to offer hope and a path to immortality.

Only Christianity exposes humanity's truly lost and hopeless state. Christianity exposes our desperate need for a Savior. There is no hope apart from God. There is no salvation apart from God. There is no goodness apart from God, as the prophet Isaiah expressed so unequivocally.

> *All we like sheep have gone astray; We have turned, every one, to his own way; And the LORD has laid on Him the iniquity of us all. (Isaiah 53:6 NKJV)*

The rituals of human religion are idolatrous. The offerings and rituals of worship offered in these religions are idolatrous. They are the foods offered to idols that Jezebel promotes. When people participate in the religious rituals and offerings of false religions, they end up forming covenants with the evil spiritual forces that empower those religions. It is impossible to participate in religious rituals without forming connections with the spiritual forces behind those religions.

Jezebel also teaches about sexual immorality. She teaches about the goodness of every form of sexual activity except one. She never teaches about the benefits of the lifelong commitment between a man and woman in marriage. She teaches about victimhood, about the injustice of biblical sexual immorality. She works to open the door to every kind of sexual sin. She teaches that biblical morality is bigotry and prejudice, that sexual sin must be celebrated by all.

Jezebel's teachings on sexuality also work to break down the God-given distinctions that exist between the sexes. Her teachings encourage men to try to become women and women to try to become men. In everything, her teachings work to undermine divinely established order and morality.

THE SEDUCTION OF JEZEBEL

Jezebel not only teaches but also seduces. The spirit of Jezebel is a spirit of sexual seduction that empowers the river of lust and uncleanness that is flowing through America today. It is the spirit behind the divas and rock stars who celebrate lust and promiscuity. It is the spirit behind the pornography that captures the minds and bodies of so many Americans.

The combination of teaching about sex and sexual seduction is simply too strong a temptation for many to resist. The seducing attraction of sexual temptation lures people towards sin while the teachings of Jezebel undermine the moral resistance that would normally help them resist that temptation. In this way, people's consciences become deadened, and they act on their sexual impulses. The more they obey the lusts of the flesh, the more enslaved to sin they become. We become the slaves of the one we obey, as the apostle Paul reminds:

> *Don't you realize that you become the slave of whatever you choose to obey? You can be a slave to sin, which leads to death, or you can choose to obey God, which leads to righteous living. (Romans 6:16 NLT)*

Sex is sacred, created by a holy God. God determined that this intimate blood covenant between two people was the way life would be formed. Sex is at the very foundation of families, at the very foundation of societies, at the very foundation of creation.

> *In the day that God created man, He made him in the likeness of God. He created them male and female, and blessed them and called them Mankind in the day they were created. (Genesis 5:2, NKJV)*

> *Therefore a man shall leave his father and mother and be joined to his wife, and they shall become one flesh (Genesis 2:24, NKJV)*

Because sex is so sacred and foundational to society, Jezebel has targeted sex as the doorway through which she can gain control over people and over societies. She turns it into something unclean and perverse, something that binds men and women to unclean spirits instead of connecting them together in a holy covenant.

THE PROPHECIES OF JEZEBEL

Jezebel calls herself a prophetess. When Jezebel tries to bring her teachings and immorality into the church, she doesn't only come as a teacher. She claims to be inspired by a higher power, and in truth she is inspirited by a higher power since her words and teachings come from an evil source.

The prophesies of Jezebel come in two forms. In the first form, Jezebel prophesies with great zeal against "injustice." Biblical prophets such as Jeremiah and Amos used their prophetic voice to confront the injustice found in their society. When Jezebel "prophesies" in the manner of these biblical prophets, she often pretends to be the voice of the powerless against the powerful. She pretends to fight for the rights of the victims against the victimizers, the oppressed against the oppressors. Her prophecy seems to carry moral authority to confront evil in our society.

The difference between Jezebel's prophets who confront evil and injustice and prophets sent from God can be found in the fruit and goals of the prophecy. A prophet sent from God will also confront the evil and injustice of society. He or she may confront individual sin such as sexual immorality as well as societal sin. The prophet or prophetess sent from God will not try to destroy the moral fabric of society but will call people towards union with a holy God. When they confront sins such as racism, they will not use the sin of racism as an excuse to try to tear down all legitimate authority. Such prophets work to build the nation and bring it back to its God-given calling and destiny, not to tear it down.

A good example of this type of prophecy can be found in the ministry of Martin Luther King, Jr. MLK confronted racism and other evils in American society. As he confronted this evil, he wasn't trying to destroy America.

He called America back to its founding principles, back to the truth that all people are created equal. He called America to a vision of unity that included all Americans.

A prophet motivated by Jezebel works to condemn America and to destroy the foundations of our society. Jezebel hates the constitution, economic freedom, religious freedom, and political freedom. She prophesies against all these things. We will speak more about Jezebel's prophetic ministry in chapters eight, nine and ten.

Jesus said of false prophets, "By their fruit you will recognize them" (Matthew 7:16 NIV). True prophets have a God-given vision for the nation and work to call the nation towards that higher vision. In contrast, Jezebel works to tear down a nation and turn it against the ways of God and righteousness of God. Prophets inspired by Jezebel are not actually seeking social justice. They are seeking the destruction of authority that resists Jezebel's control so that it can be replaced.

PROPHECY IN PENTECOSTAL AND CHARISMATIC CHURCHES

In Pentecostal and charismatic churches, Jezebel attempts to hijack the gift of prophecy. Prophecy in such churches is not usually focused on social justice but often comes in the form of personal prophecy in which people prophecy about God's plans for someone's life. When this prophecy is inspired by the Holy Spirit, it helps people know what God has called them to do, revealing His path for them more clearly.

True prophecy draws us closer to Christ. As John wrote, "the testimony of Jesus is the spirit of prophecy (Revelation 19:10)." True prophecy produces good fruit. It causes men and women to lay down their fleshly ambitions and desires, to seek the will of the Lord.

Unfortunately, Jezebel is just as skilled at hijacking this form of prophetic ministry as she is in hijacking the social justice form of prophecy. False prophets inspired by Jezebel connect to the lustful desires of a person's flesh and speak life to those desires. Personal prophecy inspired by Jezebel feeds the lusts of the flesh, encouraging people to obey the lusts of their flesh. Jezebel tells her listeners that they can have whatever they want.

Jezebel's husband King Ahab was the most privileged, wealthy, and spoiled person in his nation. Nevertheless, when Ahab couldn't get what he wanted, the vineyard belonging to Naboth, he sulked on his bed for days without eating anything. Somehow, Naboth's refusal to sell him the vineyard felt like a great offense and injustice to him. Jezebel stepped in to comfort and support Ahab in his case against Naboth, telling him:

> *Now, exercise your royal power over Israel. Get up, eat some food, and be happy. For I will give you the vineyard of Naboth the Jezreelite. (I Kings 21:7, HCSB)*

The prophesies of Jezebel are seductive because she tells people what they want to hear. She does not confront evil desires of the flesh but feeds those desires, telling people that God wants to fulfill their desires.

The prophecies of Jezebel also encourage sexual immorality. If a man lusts after another man sexually, the person inspired by Jezebel will never confront this evil desire but tell that man God made him this way and put this desire in his heart. If the man wants to be true to himself and true to the God who created him, he must obey his lust and begin a sexual relationship with the other man.

The person who lusts after money will be told that God is going to make him rich. The man who desires honor and position will be given a flattering prophecy about the greatness of his authority and calling from God. This is all false prophecy. It puffs up the flesh, feeding the pride, ambitions, and lusts of the human heart.

Chapter Six

THE WITCHCRAFT OF JEZEBEL

There is another side to Jezebel's ministry that is even darker than her prophecy, teaching, and seduction. Jezebel is a witch who uses black magic, curses, and manipulation to achieve her goals.

In 2 Kings, we read of a confrontation between Jehu, the general over Israel's armies, and King Joram, the son of Jezebel. When Jehu approached Joram, Joram asked if Jehu came in peace. Jehu responded, "How can there be peace as long as all the idolatry and witchcraft of your mother Jezebel abound?" (2 Kings 9:22, NIV). This makes clear that Queen Jezebel's practice of witchcraft was well-known within the nation of Israel.

Jezebel always works in two realms. In the seen physical realm, she attempts to gain control over governmental authority so she can use that authority to enforce her will with brute force. The biblical Jezebel used the governmental authority of King Ahab to murder Naboth and have God's prophets hunted down and killed. When Jezebel gains full control of a nation, she unleashes vicious and violent persecution against her enemies.

Jezebel also works in the spiritual realm, using curses and black magic to compel people to do her will. She uses demonic spiritual power to intimidate, oppress, and confuse her enemies. Her curses can even bring sickness and death upon those who are not protected from them. The spiritual power of Jezebel can be even more destructive than her political power.

Jezebel prophesies, teaches, and seduces. She uses her prophecy, teaching, and seduction, to bring people into covenants with the forces of darkness that are formed through sexual immorality and idolatry. These covenants connect people with demons and evil spiritual rulers.

Queen Jezebel formed covenants with the evil spiritual beings known as Baal and Asherah. In consequence, their spiritual power became available to Jezebel. When Jezebel spoke a curse, that curse was empowered by her false gods, Baal and Asherah. Her curses carried evil, demonic power to accomplish her purposes. When people are connected in covenant to evil spiritual beings, they become conduits for evil spiritual power to be released.

I have spent much of my life serving as a missionary in Africa, where belief in witches, witchcraft, and black magic remains common. In Africa, those who believe in the power of witchcraft appeal to sorcerers, witches, witchdoctors, and shamans to buy the spiritual power that can help them get what they want. A person might go to a sorcerer to buy the power to gain favor in the eyes of a boss so they will receive a promotion. A business owner might buy the power to influence his customers so they will feel compelled to buy his products. A young person might buy the power to force a potential love interest to fall in love with them.

This misuse of spiritual power is witchcraft. Witchcraft uses spiritual power to force people to do what they don't actually want to do. Witchcraft and strong manipulation are closely related. A manipulator uses a person's greed, fear, or other desires to pressure them into doing what the manipulator wants them to do. A witch uses spiritual power to pressure people into doing what they wouldn't otherwise do. In both cases, the target of the manipulator or witch feels compelled to do something he didn't freely choose to do.

But witchcraft goes beyond manipulation into the use of curses intended to destroy a target's life. In Africa, for example, a woman in a polygamous marriage might feel jealous of her husband's other wives, so she might curse those wives, speaking death and disease over them. She might go to a sorcerer to buy more powerful curses that will ensure the complete destruction of her rivals. Businesspeople and politicians do the same, buying powerful curses from sorcerers to cause their rivals to fail in their endeavors or even lose their lives.

JEZEBEL'S CURSE UPON ELIJAH

We can see the power of Jezebel's witchcraft in 1 Kings 19, where Jezebel released a curse upon Elijah, turning one of the best days of his life into the worst. Elijah had just won a great victory over the prophets of Baal and Asherah on Mount Carmel (1 Kings 18). We will study this victory in more detail in chapter sixteen. After destroying Jezebel's prophets, Elijah ran ahead of King Ahab's chariot to Jezebel's headquarters, the city of Jezreel, to confront Jezebel herself.

But upon reaching the walls of Jezreel, Elijah hesitated. Arriving behind Elijah, King Ahab went straight in to report the events of the day to Jezebel. He told her how fire had fallen from heaven and how Elijah had given the command to execute her prophets. Jezebel was enraged by the king's report. Mustering all her evil spiritual powers, she spoke the following curse over Elijah.

> *Then Jezebel sent a messenger to Elijah, saying, "So let the gods do to me, and more also, if I do not make your life as the life of one of them by tomorrow about this time." (1 Kings 19:2 NKJV)*

Jezebel's curse settled upon Elijah like a dark cloud upon his soul. The great victory Elijah had won over Jezebel's prophets seemed far away like a fading dream. Earlier in the day, Elijah had believed that Jezebel's kingdom was about to fall. Now the cold reality of Jezebel's evil power consumed Elijah's thoughts. How had he ever thought Jezebel could be defeated?

Fear gripped Elijah. If he waited one moment more, he would surely be killed, so he turned and began running as fast as he could. As fast as he'd run towards

Jezreel, he now ran away from Jezreel. He ran as a man fleeing for his life, hour after hour, as he tried to put distance between himself and Jezreel. As he ran, dark thoughts flooded his mind. *What a terrible, idolatrous nation I live in! What a hopeless, corrupted people!*

Elijah ran all the way to Beersheba, a distance of over a hundred miles from Jezreel, then set off alone across the desert. Finally, he fell exhausted to the ground under a broom tree. Discouragement and hopelessness overwhelmed him. He cried out at the sky, "It is enough! I am finished! Take my life, oh Lord, for I am no better than my fathers" (1 Kings 19:4).

With these words, Elijah fell into exhausted unconsciousness. A few hours passed. Elijah became aware of someone shaking him. A man was sitting beside him, offering him a jar of water and some cake baked on the coals of a fire that had been lit nearby.

"Wake up and eat," the man said.

Elijah had experienced many supernatural things in his time, and he knew that this man was an angel. He drank the water and ate the cake, then sank back into a peaceful sleep. Some hours later, the angel once again awakened Elijah and offered him more water and cake. The food had a very nourishing effect on Elijah. He felt life and energy returning to his body.

Elijah considered his situation. He knew the angel was likely to give him an assignment from the Lord. But Elijah didn't want another assignment. The people of Israel had witnessed such great miracles, and yet they hadn't changed. King Ahab was just as evil as he was before he saw the miracle of fire falling from heaven.

Elijah decided to leave the nation of Israel completely. They were an idolatrous people. Speaking the word of the Lord to them was a hopeless task. They never listened to God or obeyed Him. Instead, they murdered the prophets God sent to them. Elijah had had enough!

So even as new strength filled his body, Elijah set off on a journey out of the land of Israel. For forty days, he traveled as fast as he could into the wilderness all the way to Mount Horeb, the mountain of God, where Moses had met with the Lord. There God met with Elijah and gave him instructions. We will look at the rest of this story in chapters sixteen and seventeen.

WITCHCRAFT IS REAL

The witchcraft of Jezebel is real. Jezebel's curse brought the great prophet Elijah into a condition of deep, suicidal depression on the same day that he'd won a great victory over Jezebel's prophets. The same man who had walked up Mount Carmel with such great faith, boldness, and authority literally ran for forty days from Jezebel without faith or hope, begging God to take his life. If the curse of Jezebel can turn one of the bravest, most powerful prophets of God in all of human history into such a despairing wreck of a man, then we can be assured that the power of Jezebel's witchcraft is real.

When witchcraft is sent against a believer, they lose their clarity, their ability to take action. Witchcraft settles upon them like a dark cloud just as it did upon the prophet Elijah. They feel intimidated, confused, and depressed. Instead of seeing the power of God that is available to them, they can only see the overwhelming power of the evil one. The situation appears hopeless, and they feel isolated and alone just as Elijah did. The power of the enemy appears so overwhelming and unstoppable that resistance seems futile.

And as faith evaporates, fear kicks into action. Fear is kind of a negative faith, the opposite of faith. Just as real faith turns situations in a positive direction and releases God's power to work things in our favor, fear releases the power of the evil one to twist a situation in a negative direction. As a person becomes terrified and intimidated by the evil one, the evil one gains authority over that person and begins pulling them down a dark path. When you fear the worst, the worst can actually begin to happen to you.

The purpose of these curses is to make things seem so hopeless that nobody will try to resist Jezebel. Just as it did with Elijah, depression and confusion can cripple the man or woman who hopes to take action against Jezebel. Those facing Jezebel today will face intimidation and persecution from governmental forces aligned with Jezebel. They will face the accusations and manipulations of Jezebel's servants just as Naboth did. And they will face the same witchcraft that Elijah faced.

The fight with Jezebel is ultimately a spiritual battle, and the spirit of Jezebel uses evil spiritual powers to accomplish her purposes. The person who hopes to overcome Jezebel must become effective in spiritual warfare.

TRUE WORSHIP

Most importantly, a person who faces Jezebel must be a true worshiper of God. Jezebel works to trap a nation in the false worship of her idols. She also seeks to capture the focus and attention of God's servants so that they can only see the darkness surrounding them and not the light of God. This is what happened to Elijah when he took his eyes off of God and became focused on the darkness that filled the nation of Israel. When he did this, he came under the full weight of Jezebel's curse. He became so focused on the darkness that he became incapable of taking the effective action needed to combat Jezebel. God then instructed him to anoint his successors, men who could take steps in faith.

Worship is very, very important. In true worship, we see the Lord and worship the Lord. In true worship, the reality of God's greatness and goodness fills our mind, emotions, heart, and soul. In true worship, we begin to see the Lord as He is.

The power of the Lord is much stronger than all of Jezebel's witchcraft. The word of the Lord is much stronger than all of Jezebel's curses. A single person who walks in unity with the Spirit of the Lord walks in greater authority than all the servants of Jezebel put together. The plans of the Lord will ultimately succeed while the plans of Jezebel will come to an end.

This is ultimate reality. The dark clouds of oppression released by Jezebel's witchcraft seem to be reality when they settle upon one's consciousness. But ultimately, the depressing, hopeless thoughts released by these curses are just deception. The servants of the Lord will be triumphant over Jezebel.

The end of Jezebel is written. Elijah prophesied about Jezebel: "The dogs shall eat Jezebel by the wall of Jezreel" (1 Kings 21:23, NKJV). And surely enough, in the end dogs ate the body of Jezebel next to the wall of Jezreel.

Elijah prophesied about Ahab's offspring, including the children born to Jezebel: "Behold, I will bring calamity on you. I will take away your posterity, and will cut off from Ahab every male in Israel, both bond and free" (1 Kings 21:21, NKJV). And surely enough, Ahab's descendants were destroyed by Jehu.

Jesus prophesied about the spirit of Jezebel: "I will cast her into a sickbed, and those who commit adultery with her into great tribulation, unless they repent of their deeds. I will kill her children with death" (Revelation 2:22-23). And surely enough, Jezebel and her entire system will soon come to an end. The kingdom of our God is coming. The earth will be filled with the knowledge of the glory of the LORD as the waters cover the sea (Habakkuk 2:14).

The true worshiper knows in his heart that God's plans will succeed and all the works of Jezebel will be destroyed. The true worshiper is able to meet with the Lord even when clouds of oppression are sent against him.

God is seeking these worshipers who worship Him in spirit and truth. He will use these worshipers to take action against the forces of Jezebel during the dark days that will afflict the earth at the end of this age. They will keep their eyes on the Lord. They will not be intimidated or oppressed by the witchcraft of Jezebel. They will stay connected to the Lord and to His instructions even when the curses of Jezebel are sent against them. They will remove the influence of Jezebel from the earth.

We will study this restoration of true worship and true worshipers in more detail in chapter twenty.

Chapter Seven

JEZEBEL'S SCHOOLS

The spirit of Jezebel is a control spirit with a plan to control every part of society. The foundations of Jezebel's authority in America can be found in America's schools. Jezebel takes control of schools and uses them to train her disciples so that they can spread her influence and control throughout the nation.

What does such a school look like? In a school controlled by Jezebel, American students learn to worship the idol of self. They learn to despise God-given authority. They learn to celebrate what is perverse and profane and to despise all that is godly. And from these schools come America's leaders in every field, discipled in the ways of Jezebel.

In a school controlled by Jezebel, biblical Christian faith is mocked, ridiculed, and condemned. It is a school in which Christian students are afraid to admit that they are Christian. The apostle Paul writes:

> *For the flesh lusts against the Spirit, and the Spirit against the flesh; and these are contrary to one another . . . Now the works of the flesh are evident, which are adultery, fornication, uncleanness, lewdness, idolatry, sorcery, hatred, contentions, jealousies, outbursts of wrath, selfish ambitions, dissensions, heresies, envy, murders, drunkenness, revelries, and the like; of which I tell you beforehand, just as I also told you in time past,*

*that those who practice such things will not inherit the kingdom of God.
(Galatians 5:17-21, NKJV)*

Biblical Christianity dares to declare that humanity is a fallen race, that we are not inherently good. Biblical Christian faith exposes the sinfulness of humankind's selfish desires, the works of the flesh. Biblical Christianity teaches us that the lusts of the flesh do not come from God. They are contrary to the spirit of God, and to the righteousness of God. These basic Christian truths are continually under attack in a school that is controlled by Jezebel.

MORAL AUTONOMY

In a school controlled by Jezebel, students are taught to believe in an extreme form of moral autonomy. Morality does not come from God. The autonomous individual is able to decide what is right and what is wrong without any help from God, church, society, or religion. Inevitably, whatever such a person likes or desires is thought to be morally good, and whatever they dislike is considered morally wrong. Anything or anyone who tries to keep others from doing what they want is evil. Anyone who tells them that they shouldn't simply obey their sexual desires without constraint is morally evil.

The individual is free from the constraints of every authority that they do not choose. They are free from the moral authority of parents, who have no right to tell them what to do. They are free from the moral authority of the church, which has no right to tell them that what they want to do is wrong. The individual is able to decide what is right and what is wrong without any interference from others.

In reality, these students are pawns controlled by Jezebel. Their autonomous moral authority is honored only so long as they make choices in alignment with Jezebel's purposes. If such students should choose to follow biblical morality, they would be immediately condemned.

SEXUALITY

Naturally, such views have enormous repercussions on the sexual lives of American students. When Jezebel controls a school, students are taught the value of sexual immorality. They are taught that the lusts of their flesh are sacred and should be obeyed. They are taught that every kind of sexual experimentation is good. They are taught that anyone who would tell them to restrict their sexual expression in any way is full of hatred and intolerance.

In Jezebel's schools, students are actually trained in sexual immorality. They are taught how to engage in different forms of sexual activity, including anal and oral sex, in a way that mitigates negative consequences of that activity. They are taught about birth control and sexually transmitted diseases.

In such a school, sexual immorality doesn't just flow from teaching in a classroom. The spirit of Jezebel seduces people into committing sexual immorality (Revelations 2:20). In a school controlled by Jezebel, it becomes normal for students to engage in sexual activity with one another. Parties and social activities associated with the school are highly sexualized with students engaging in random lust and alcohol-fueled sexual "hookups."

In such a school, Jezebel controls the value system, what is wrong and what is right. She controls the social order of the school. High status students are those who are promiscuous. Popular girls engage in sexual activity with many partners. Popular boys do the same. Students text each other with sexualized messages and photos of their body parts. Nearly all are involved in pornography, and they freely discuss all kinds of sexual depravity.

In such a school, biblical sexual morality is ridiculed and condemned. Students feel ostracized if they don't participate in sexual activity with their classmates. Those who believe sex should be reserved for marriage are made to feel ashamed of their convictions. Students are taught that the Bible is filled with hate speech targeted against gays, lesbians, and those who engage in promiscuity.

If this description of a school controlled by Jezebel sounds familiar, it is because Jezebel has gained almost total control over America's public schools and many of the private ones as well. Christian parents who resist the influence of Jezebel have often found it necessary to remove their children from the public school system.

REPLACING THE KNOWLEDGE OF GOD

Jezebel replaces worship of the Creator with worship of her idol. We can see this replacement in the changes that have taken place at Harvard University, which has been ranked as the world's top university. Harvard was originally established to train ministers of the gospel of Jesus Christ. Its motto was "Truth for Christ and the Church." Today that motto has been changed to just "Veritas" (Truth).

Harvard has over forty chaplains representing various religions. In August 2021, Harvard's chaplains elected Greg Epstein to be their new president. In this choice, the chaplains revealed the religious system that is in place at Harvard. Greg Epstein is a humanist chaplain and an atheist. Although Greg doesn't believe in God, he does believe in something. He believes in the idol of self.

"We don't look to a god for answers," says Epstein. "We are each other's answers."

Students at Harvard and most of America's educational institutions are not taught the limits of science. They are not taught that nobody has ever been able to provide a reasonable explanation of how a cell can come into being through random events. They are not taught that evolutionary processes simply cannot explain the mind-blowing complexity of the molecular machinery of life. They are not taught that scientists have never provided even a remotely believable explanation for how "evolution" created our own consciousness. They are not taught that random chance cannot explain any part of the universe we live in but that all scientific evidence points to the work of a creative intelligence far beyond our ability to comprehend.

At Harvard and at most of America's educational institutions, students are taught that there is no creator of the universe and no creator of life. As the knowledge of God is removed from students' lives, the idol of self can take the place of God.

Chapter Eight

JEZEBEL'S CRITICAL THEORIES

As Jezebel uses America's schools to build her system, she doesn't just break down belief and worship of the Creator. She must also break down and delegitimize every form of authority that carries authority given by the Creator. A school under the control of Jezebel will systematically teach its students to despise legitimate God-given authority. Students will be taught to despise the authority of churches and parents. They will be taught to despise biblical Christianity and the Bible itself. In many cases, they will be taught to despise their own nation. The American system of limited constitutional government limits Jezebel's plans to control the nation, so she works to turn students against that system.

To do this, Jezebel uses a weapon known as *critical theory*. Critical theory is an academic social theory that attempts to dig beneath the surface of America's culture and social life so that hidden biases and injustices of our society can be exposed. Critical theory takes many forms, but all of them help work towards a common goal—the delegitimization and condemnation of virtually every part of American history and society.

This method of studying America's literature, culture, and social life has achieved a suffocating level of control over many fields of study in America's institutes of higher learning, including literature, sociology, psychology, legal studies, women's studies, and many others.

DEFINITION OF CRITICAL THEORY

According to the Stanford Encyclopedia of Philosophy, a "critical" theory may be distinguished from a "traditional" theory in its purpose. A theory is critical to the extent that it seeks human "emancipation from slavery," acts as a "liberating ... influence," and works "to create a world which satisfies the needs and powers of [human beings]."

In other words, critical theorists identify different forms of slavery and seek to liberate people from them. Critical theory is used to expose the hidden forms of injustice in our society.

You might think our society is relatively just compared to many other societies. Critical theory will teach you the error of your ways. Critical theorists will teach you that American society is irredeemably racist, irredeemably sexist, and irredeemably biased against those who aren't part of your heteronormative, cis-gendered, privileged, and institutionally racist world.

THE MARXIST ROOTS OF CRITICAL THEORY

The first critical theorists were Marxists, and the first critical theory was critical Marxist theory. Marxists followed the teachings of Karl Marx, the nineteenth-century German philosopher who taught the world about class struggle. Marx believed that humanity's core conflict was between the ruling class (bourgeoisie) who owned the means of production and the working class. He believed conflict between the two classes would eventually lead to the destruction of the capitalist system and rise of the "dictatorship of the proletariat," under which the working class would control the means of production, inequality and injustice would cease, and the world would enter into a communist utopia.

Marxists succeeded in bringing violent revolution to such nations as China and the USSR, destroying the existing governmental and economic systems and instituting their new communist system, supposedly on behalf of the workers. These communist revolutions destroyed the lives of millions of people and brought to power brutal, dictatorial governments that created far more injustice than the governments that they replaced.

Many who resisted these governments were sent to the horrific slave labor camps of Siberia and other places. Many others were simply murdered. It is estimated that approximately fifteen million people were executed, starved, or worked to death in the former USSR. It is estimated that more than fifty million people were executed, starved, or worked to death in communist China. Quite simply, the disciples of Karl Marx are responsible for building some of the most murderous, oppressive, and unjust governmental and economic systems the world has ever seen.

In Europe, some Marxists realized they were not going to stir up Europe's workers in a violent revolution against their governments. Instead, these Marxists focused their attention upon the infiltration and control of Europe's educational system, through which they hoped to gradually undermine European society from within.

In Frankfurt, Germany, a group of Marxists founded a think-tank called the Institute of Social Research, later known as the Frankfurt School. This Marxist think-tank was the birthplace of critical theory. After the Nazis rose to power in 1933, the scholars who invented critical theory left Germany and moved to America, where they established themselves in Columbia University. They began to focus their theories on the hidden injustices of American society instead of Europe.

Critical Marxist theory separates everyone into two categories—the oppressors and the oppressed. In the case of Marxists and critical Marxist theory, the oppressors are the bourgeoise, the ruling class, those who own the businesses and the means of production. The oppressed are the workers, the peasants, those who own less than their rulers.

Both groups are part of a society in which the belief systems and cultural norms of that society always work for the benefit of the oppressors. The oppressed come to believe that the inequality and injustice they experience in their society is actually justified, so they participate in their own oppression. But through careful training, the oppressed working classes can begin to understand just how unjust and unfair their society actually is. The economic system always works in favor of the capitalist owners of the means of production and against the workers. The culture, the literature, in fact every part of society is filled with bias and injustice that always works in favor of the capitalist oppressors.

Is the American economic system really so unjust? It would be difficult to find a group in human history that has enjoyed more prosperity than modern Americans. Americans live lives of luxury compared to other times and places. Even the poorest Americans have smartphones and other luxuries that even kings could not imagine a hundred years ago. Even the poorest Americans struggle with the afflictions of overabundance. Poor people in America don't die of starvation but of diabetes and other afflictions of overeating and overabundance.

Compared to many nations, there has always been a very high level of economic mobility in America. A large percentage of America's poor are able to work their way into the middle class and above. For almost two hundred fifty years, millions of people have flocked to America because of the economic and religious freedom they find here. They are still coming to America for that reason, legally and illegally. Some risk everything to get here.

I met a man who told me his story of how he illegally entered America. "Raul" crossed our southern border with a group of fourteen others. The leader who was guiding them through the desert was captured by ICE agents. The rest fled into the desert, where they became lost. One by one, they began to die of dehydration. Only Raul and one other escaped the desert alive. One week later, Raul was earning twenty-nine dollars an hour laying driveways in Connecticut. Today he is prospering financially as he builds a better life for himself and his family.

I have ministered to thousands of illegal immigrants who come to the United States from Latin America. For the most part, these immigrants don't come to America because they expect government handouts. They come to America because of freedom. Some of them are fleeing nations such as Venezuela, where the socialist government has destroyed economic freedom. Others are fleeing the brutality of drug cartels. They come to America because they believe that in America they will be free to build a better life. They believe that if they work hard and work smart, they can prosper and succeed without the fear of having their earnings stolen by violent men. And they do succeed. I know many who came to America in poverty, and have prospered here. Quite a few have become millionaires.

CRITICAL RACE THEORY

There is more than one way to determine who is an oppressor and who is oppressed. Other critical theories soon followed on the heels of critical Marxist theory, dividing up society in different ways. Critical race theory divides people by race. The oppressors are the whites, who have formed a society with values and norms that always benefit white people. Ethnic minorities are the oppressed. They grow up in a society controlled by their oppressors.

Ethnic minorities might think that if they work hard and work smart, they might be able to work their way up in American society and lead successful, prosperous lives. They might think Jim Crow, segregated schools, and other obviously racist laws are a thing of the past and America is full of opportunities for every ethnic group. But in America's universities, critical race theorists are there to teach them just how wrong they are.

According to critical race theorists, the only acceptable explanation for inequalities of wealth, income, or education that exist between different ethnic groups in American society is racism. Even when American society gets rid of overtly racist laws, the norms and values of that society continue to work in favor of the oppressors. Critical race theorists work tirelessly to show that America is irredeemably racist, its culture is racist, its institutions are racist, its schools are racist, its speech is racist. It's almost as if the critical race theorists hate America and believe that it should be destroyed.

Is institutional racism really the only possible explanation for inequality experienced between races? Some ethnic groups seem to be almost obsessed with the value of education and hard work while others are not. In some ethnic groups, the family structures remain intact while in others they have disintegrated. Levels of criminality are much higher in some ethnic groups than others. These differences all have enormous impacts on the financial well-being of different ethnic groups. Are all these differences due to hidden biases and institutional racism?

Asian Americans certainly experienced discrimination in American history. American citizens with Japanese ancestry were placed in internment camps during World War II. Yet in spite of that historical oppression, Asian Americans have risen to the top of American society with significantly higher average incomes than their white counterparts. According to the US Census Bureau, in 2018 the mean annual income of Indian Americans was $119,858. Taiwanese Americans, Chinese Americans, and Japanese Americans all earned significantly higher incomes than did white Americans, whose mean household income was $67,937. If the present system is so biased against ethnic minorities, how is it possible that Asian Americans have succeeded so dramatically?

It's not only Asian Americans who are prospering in America. African immigrants are also doing quite well. As I have traveled and worked in Africa, I have frequently been impressed by the strong, middle class value system that has become established in Africa's rising middle class. Members of Africa's middle class typically place an enormous emphasis on the importance of hard work, education, and strong families. And when members of this middle class emigrate to America, they usually prosper.

According to the US Census Bureau, in 2018 the mean annual income of a Nigerian American household was $68,658, and for Ghanian Americans $69,343. If the institutions of America are so completely racist, why are African immigrants to America earning more money than their white, American counterparts?

CRITICAL FEMINIST AND LGBT THEORY

Critical feminist theory analyzes society in a similar way. According to critical feminist theorists, American society is a patriarchy that always works for the benefit of patriarchal males. The oppressors are the male members of the patriarchy while the oppressed are the women who suffer under the patriarchy. Although many women share the same value system of the males who control this patriarchal system, they are deceived. They need to be woken up, to become "woke."

One of the proofs of patriarchal oppression offered by critical feminist theorists is the gender pay gap, the fact that women earn only seventy-eight percent of what their male counterparts earn in the same professions. In fact, this gender pay gap has been repeatedly debunked. The income disparity between men and women completely disappears when the years worked and hours per week are factored into the equation. Quite simply, women are making different life choices than men, and these choices affect income. They are not staying in the workforce as many years as men nor working as many hours as men.

In America's universities, women's studies programs study critical feminist theory. They learn about the hidden value systems of the patriarchy. They learn that they are in fact victims. They learn that literature, culture, speech, and societal norms work to form a system in which their oppression is normalized. In fact, American society is irredeemably patriarchal and sexist. It should be destroyed so a better, more egalitarian system can be constructed in its place.

Critical LGBT theorists have also gained great influence and control over American universities. Critical LGBT theory divides American society into the oppressed and oppressors. The oppressors are the heterosexual, cis-gendered persons who have built a society that always works for the benefit of heterosexual, cis-gendered persons. The oppressed are the members of the LGBT community, who are oppressed within American heteronormative society. They are oppressed by Christians who still hold on to oppressive, outdated beliefs that sex outside of heterosexual marriage is sin.

FREEDOM AND INEQUALITY

When people are free to make choices, they make different choices with different outcomes. When people are free to pursue happiness as stated in the Declaration of Independence, they pursue happiness in different ways. One person pursues happiness by working extreme hours and making a lot of money. He has the right to do this. Another person believes money is not the ultimate means to happiness and prioritizes time spent with family. Another person values free time and prioritizes hobbies. Some may spend their life in spiritual pursuits, believing that in seeking God's will they will find true meaning, happiness, and eternal reward.

Do we need political activists to tell us that one is right and the other is wrong? Do we need political activists to tell us that the one who prioritizes something other than money is the victim of injustice? Who are they to judge one's life choices, one's pursuit of happiness?

Where there is freedom, there will never be financial equality because some people will choose to pursue wealth more than others while others will decide there are things in life worth more than earthly wealth. Critical theorists are blind to these truths. They measure the financial wealth of different groups, and when they find differences in this wealth, they declare that these differences can only be explained by injustice.

Chapter Nine

THE OPPRESSION AND HYPOCRISY OF CRITICAL THEORY

Critical theory in its different forms has gained such control over America's universities that people are afraid to say anything that is not in complete agreement with this theory. It is dangerous to say anything that can be interpreted as even remotely negative about one of critical theory's "oppressed" groups. Untenured university employees can lose their jobs very easily. Tenured professors usually need to prove their loyalty to critical theory long before they receive tenure.

Not only have people become terrified of speaking anything that might be interpreted negatively by an oppressed group but of speaking anything positive about groups deemed to be oppressors. Since critical theorists have determined the foundations of America are incurably racist and oppressive, it simply isn't acceptable to talk about positive things our founding fathers accomplished. It isn't acceptable to speak of opportunities available to American citizens of all races. It isn't acceptable to say anything positive about traditional gender roles or Christianity or the Constitution of the United States. It isn't acceptable say anything positive about the times Americans stood for freedom and defeated the forces of Nazism, communism, and slavery. Everything about America must be condemned repeatedly and endlessly.

Critical theorists have an almost allergic reaction when they hear something positive about our nation, our founding fathers, or Christianity in general. They immediately and forcefully begin to recite the most negative moments related to those topics. Say something positive about Christianity? Prepare to listen to an account of the most brutal moments of the Crusades. Say something positive about the constitution or founding fathers? Prepare for a lecture on slavery. If you say something positive about an oppressor, you must be on the side of the oppressors.

Critical theorists have decided that evangelical Christians belong in the oppressor category. If anything positive is said about them, people need to be reeducated to know just how hypocritical and evil evangelical Christians really are.

Of course, it seems ridiculous to accuse evangelical Christians of being privileged members of society. America's top educational institutions, corporations, and newsrooms are dominated by Jezebel's disciples. Evangelical Christians are rarely permitted to have a voice or a place in America's corridors of power and influence. Yet Jezebel convinces her students that white evangelicals are a privileged segment of society's oppressors.

In this way, political correctness rules the universities of America and increasingly rules American society in general. Just as communists fighting oppression formed some of the most oppressive governments the world has ever seen, critical theorists who specialize in fighting oppression are responsible for some of the worst oppression in America today.

Critical theory is an extremely divisive and destructive ideology. The person trained in critical theory will never have a balanced view of American history, Christianity, male-female relationships, or anything else. Critical theory teaches its adherents to focus relentlessly on the negative aspects of oppressor groups and the oppressive history of a nation controlled by the oppressors. They are taught to always blame those they have identified as the oppressors and never the oppressed. It is an extremely one-sided view that poisons those who are trained in it.

The truth is, there is good and evil in every person and in every group. There is plenty of evil and hypocrisy in every segment of humanity. It is impossible to clearly separate humans by groups into "oppressor" and "oppressed." All have sinned, and fallen short of the glory of God.

NEGATIVE ELEMENTS OF AMERICAN SOCIETY

If critical theory is so destructive, how should we view American society and American history? Should we cover up the negative elements of our history and only focus on the positive?

At the present moment, there is such an imbalance in many of America's universities, such a laser-like focus on the failures of America, that it is more beneficial for the emphasis to shift in a more positive direction than to endlessly repeat the negative. If America has a future, it must identify the things in its history that are worth saving. It must focus on the good things in our nation and not only the evil and injustice. Even left of political center Americans understood this in times past. Martin Luther King and other civil rights activists demonstrated a deep love for their nation and worked to bring us together as one people.

But this doesn't mean the negative side should be covered up. We also need to recognize the mistakes, hypocrisy, and evil in our history if we hope to go forward. For example, many of America's founding fathers were deeply hypocritical on the issue of slavery, and their compromise and hypocrisy found its way into our nation's constitution. The most serious of these were the compromises made with the institution of slavery, particularly the Three-Fifths Compromise and Fugitive Slave Clause. The founding documents declared that all men are created equal and given the gift of liberty by God, yet those same documents made provisions for the ownership of slaves.

While those compromises seemed necessary at the time to unite slave-owning states with states that forbade slave ownership, America paid a high cost in blood for its compromise. During the Civil War, Abraham Lincoln came to understand that America was paying a price for its sin of enslaving others. In his second inaugural address as the Civil War dragged on, Lincoln stated:

> *Fondly do we hope—fervently do we pray—that this mighty scourge of war may speedily pass away. Yet, if God wills that it continue until all the wealth piled by the bond-men's two hundred and fifty years of unrequited toil shall be sunk, and until every drop of blood drawn with the lash shall be paid by another drawn by the sword, as was said three thousand years ago, so still it must be said, "the judgments of the Lord are true and righteous altogether."*

In other words, if every drop of blood shed because of slavery needed to be paid for with blood shed in the Civil War, this price would be a form of God's righteous judgment upon our nation. Though hundreds of thousands of lives were lost, these compromises in our nation's foundations were finally removed. Thank God for those who gave their lives so this could happen. Thank God for those who cared enough to fight for freedom. Thank God for those who fought for civil rights a hundred years later.

Because such a great price was paid to rebuild our nation's foundations, we should value those foundations all the more. We reap the benefits today of what they did and should highly value what has been given to us.

Yet today critical theorists completely despise the foundation of this nation. They want to uproot the foundation and start over because of flaws in that foundation. They want to focus like a laser on the sins of racism and slavery so they can justify their complete destruction of our nations' foundations. They claim that America is irredeemably racist, that its institutions are racist, that nothing of value has been gained by those who fought against these evils at such a high cost.

It's kind of like buying a house, and discovering that one of the main beams is rotten. At great expense, you pay workers to tear off the roof, replace that main beam, and rebuild the roof. Yet after the work is done, someone wants to claim that your house is worthless and should be destroyed because its beam needed to be replaced. They bring a wrecking ball and start screaming at you to get out of the way.

UNRIGHTEOUS JUDGES

As we look at the destructive influence of critical theory in American schools, it is important to realize what is really happening. Critical theorists judge America very, very harshly. They condemn America and American society because of its sins of injustice, oppression, and racism. But who are the ones doing the judging? Do they have the right to judge America? Jesus said:

> *Judge not, that you be not judged. For with what judgment you judge, you will be judged; and with the measure you use, it will be measured back to you. And why do you look at the speck in your brother's eye, but do not consider the plank in your own eye? Or how can you say to your brother, "Let me remove the speck from your eye"; and look, a plank is in your own eye? Hypocrite! First remove the plank from your own eye, and then you will see clearly to remove the speck from your brother's eye. (Matthew 7:1-5, NKJV)*

Who are the ones behind the spread of critical theory in America? At the root of critical theory is Marxism and critical Marxist theory. Marxists are the sworn enemies of America. They hate America, the American constitution, and American freedom. They hate America's free economy and freedom of religion. These are the ones teaching our children. These are the ones judging and condemning our society.

Are these Marxists morally qualified to judge America in this way? Marxists condemn America for the sin of slavery that took place over a hundred-fifty years ago. Yet today, Marxist controlled countries are still engaged in slavery. Chinese Marxists still operate slave labor camps where Uighurs and other minority groups are brutally treated. North Korea is even worse.

RIGHTEOUS JUDGMENT

Jesus also said: "Judge not according to appearances, but judge with righteous judgment" (John 7:24, NKJV). So what is righteous judgment?

If you have a child who did some foolish things when he was five years old, would it be okay to constantly remind the child of what he'd done years after the fact or tell him he is evil and worthless because of those past events? Is that righteous judgment? Of course not. That would be child abuse. Such behavior would only be done by someone who deeply hated and resented that child. That resentful person should never be allowed anywhere near the child.

Who has the God-given authority to discipline and correct a child? Isn't it the parents, who deeply love the child, believe in the child, and would even give their lives for the child? Aren't they the ones put in place by God to discipline a child?

These are the principles of righteous judgment. Righteous judgment can only be brought by those who deeply love those to whom they bring correction. Righteous judgment is correction, not condemnation. The ones whom God sends to bring correction to America are those who deeply love this country and believe in this country just as parents love and believe in the future of their child.

Those who would judge righteously must first be morally qualified to judge. They must not be deeply compromised in the areas where they want to bring change and correction. They must first remove the log from their own eye before trying to correct someone else.

Marxists are the least qualified persons to judge anything or anyone in America because of the extreme injustice, slavery, and mass murder that has taken place in every nation ruled by Marxists. May every Marxist be removed from America's institutions of higher learning. May they be judged in the same way they have judged America and reap what they've sowed unless they repent.

The spirit of Jezebel hates America, not because of the injustices that have taken place in America but because of the good that still remains in America.

She condemns the American governmental and societal system because she wants to replace them with her own system. She works with the Marxists because Marxists always work to build extremely oppressive, controlling governmental systems once they achieve power. The spirit of Jezebel needs such a government to build her system and to enforce the worship of her idol.

May those who teach American history to American students be those who actually love America. May they teach students about what is good in America. May those who want to correct America be those who actually believe in America. May our teachers expose and correct the sins of America in a way that actually brings about positive change.

May God give grace to those who love this country and build upon its foundations. May God give grace to those who honor the fathers and mothers of this nation, those who fought for freedom in every generation. May everyone who desires to despise and remove the foundations of this nation so that they can institute an evil and oppressive system of government be defeated.

Chapter Ten

JEZEBEL'S ARMY OF RAGE

Jezebel has a rage-filled army she uses to attack and intimidate anyone who resists her plans. For the most part, this army receives its basic training in America's institutes of higher learning. There the army learns they are victims of a society controlled by white oppressors, heterosexual oppressors, Christian oppressors, and cis-gendered oppressors. They are victims of the patriarchy, colonizers, a racially biased justice system. All of this injustice produces rage, which is the fuel that feeds Jezebel's army of victims.

UNLIKELY VICTIMS

American college students might seem unlikely victims. These aren't the Americans who enter the workforce at a young age, learning to work long, hard hours as they build themselves a future. They aren't usually facing the pressure of raising a young family.

On the contrary, American college students are among the most privileged groups on this planet. They live in a sheltered environment, protected from the real world. They live on incredible campuses filled with more amenities than the average country club. They are coddled and pampered. They are protected from opinions and views that might disturb them in any way.

Compared to the schools of Europe and many other parts of the world, the classes are easy and graduation requirements modest. Grade inflation ensures even a modest effort will enable one to obtain an impressive GPA. The limited workload permits makes it possible for one to indulge in a myriad of parties and social activities.

In the midst of this abundance, American college students are taught that they are the victims of oppression and injustice. They learn to value their identity as victims. They learn how to obtain membership in the different oppressed groups as defined by the critical theorists.

It might seem strange that such a privileged group could be so filled with rage about the injustice they have suffered. But this is the work of Jezebel. Jezebel needs soldiers who believe they have been terribly mistreated. Jezebel uses the wounds of these soldiers to channel their sense of rage and injustice in the direction she wants it to go.

Sometimes the wounds of these soldiers are the result of real injustice that Jezebel manipulates for her own purposes. Sometimes the injustice is imaginary as in the case of Ahab when Naboth's refusal to sell him the vineyard led him to an emotional breakdown. Sometimes the wounds are self-inflicted. Wherever the wounds come from, Jezebel has proven capable of using them for her purposes.

MANIPULATING AMERICA'S WOUNDS

Jezebel "calls herself a prophetess" (Revelation 2:20). In her role as social justice warrior, she pretends to walk in the footsteps of the biblical prophets who confronted injustice. She pretends to be the voice of the oppressed against the oppressors, the powerless against the powerful.

This is Jezebel at her most deceitful. She preys upon the wounded people of a society, the victims and the broken. She pretends to stand against injustice, racism, and sexism. She pretends to be for women's rights, minority rights,

African-American rights, and LGBT rights. She pretends to be the modern manifestation of a long line of warriors who fought against injustice. She pretends to be the modern manifestation of the abolitionists who fought against slavery, of the suffragettes who fought for women's right to vote.

This is what she cloaks herself with. Yet her ultimate goal is not to get rid of racism, sexism, or homophobia. Jezebel's ultimate goal is to control everything and everyone, to build a system of oppression in America worse than anything that came before it.

Jezebel uses the wounds and resentments of the people to create an army that will fight with her against the existing social order. She convinces her wounded warriors that the existing social order is an abomination. She convinces minorities that America and its constitution is completely racist, that it cannot be reformed but must be replaced.

Method actors learn how to focus the hurt and anger they've experienced in life into the roles they play as actors. For example, a scene might require an actor to show bitterness towards someone who betrayed him. The method actor will dig into his childhood to find an example of someone who actually betrayed him. He remembers how his father left him when he was just three years old,. He captures the pain of that event, bringing genuine emotion into his acting performance.

Yet this actor is just acting. He isn't expressing his anger against the father who left him but against another actor like himself. In a similar way, Jezebel manipulates the pain from past wounds and experiences. She helps to transform that pain into rage which can be channeled in the direction she desires. Usually, the target on whom Jezebel focuses this anger had nothing to do with causing the wound in the first place.

Nobody can deny the deep pain African Americans experienced under two hundred fifty years of slavery and a racist controlling system. Families were ripped apart, people tortured, men and women bought and sold like cattle. But Jezebel has no interest in healing those wounds. She works to infect those wounds and make them more painful than ever. She wants to channel that anger towards the destruction of those who would resist her.

In particular, Jezebel wants to destroy anything that is righteous, anything that is truly Christian, anything that represents godly authority in a land. Who better to attack godly authority than those who have suffered under the abuses of those in authority? Who better to attack America as being irredeemably racist, hypocritical, and oppressive than those whose ancestors suffered as slaves in America?

Consider the young man who is mocked by his classmates for his effeminate mannerisms during childhood, becoming the victim of cruel jokes and social ostracism. As time goes on, this young man embraces a homosexual identity and becomes involved in promiscuous homosexual behavior. He unites with other gays and lesbians. The pain this man experienced in his childhood fuels his rage against anyone who would dare to question the righteousness of his behavior. It is easy for Jezebel to manipulate this young man's pain and use him as a soldier in her army.

Perhaps a woman has a dominant, abusive father. When she leaves home and enters college, she falls prey to feminist teachers who lecture her about the evils of patriarchy. This woman becomes convinced that the main problem in society is the male dominated power structures. Everywhere she looks, she starts to see the evils of patriarchy and resolves to fight against them. She carries her anger into her career and into the church she attends.

The problem is not masculinity in general. God created masculinity different from femininity and wants men to be masculine. But He wants them to use their God-given masculine strength for positive purposes. In reality, strong male leaders do not abuse women but protect and empower them. If I am a strong man, I protect my wife and daughters. I provide a secure environment in which they can flourish. I use my strength and authority to help my wife and daughters succeed in life. Strong men do not oppress women. Weak men oppress women.

The woman who was wounded by a domineering, controlling father becomes vulnerable to a hijacking attempt by Jezebel. Jezebel will try to use her to attack men who stand in their God-given authority. She will oppose the authority of a father to bring discipline to his children. She will oppose the authority of a president to take action to protect his country. She will oppose strong men who are doing what they are supposed to be doing.

THE MORAL SUPERIORITY OF VICTIMS

In America's schools, students learn more than victimhood and oppression. They also learn about their own moral superiority. Membership in an oppressed group grants one automatic moral superiority over those who are in oppressor groups. The more oppressed groups in which one can claim membership, the better. These memberships work in a cumulative manner, each one increasing one's moral superiority over non-members. Critical theorists call this accumulation of victim identities and moral authority "intersectionality."

White, upper-middle-class Anglo-Saxon Protestants don't easily fit into most of critical theory's categories of victimhood. However, the pressure to embrace victimhood is so strong that even the most privileged Americans will take up the cause. They might not be female, black, or gay, but they can become the champions of these oppressed minorities if they embrace the right politics. In this way, they can share in the moral superiority of the oppressed groups. And from their newly elevated moral position, they can despise and condemn the corruption, ignorance, and injustice of American society.

In Jezebel's schools, victims reign supreme with unassailable moral authority. Students are taught that one of the worst things they can ever to is to blame the victim. Victims are taught that they don't need to take responsibility for their own actions. The oppressors are to blame for everything.

If you raise up a class of victims with unassailable moral authority who can never be called to account for their own actions, you have created an army that can be used to tear down and attack many things. Jezebel manipulates victims. She takes their side and speaks for them. She uses their moral authority to attack the legitimate authority she wants to tear down.

It's kind of like watching an action movie in which the movie's producers prepare the viewer to enjoy the onscreen slaughter of dozens of people. Before the slaughter commences, the hero suffers injustice at the hands of the bad guys. When he starts killing people, the audience cheers him on because they have been emotionally conditioned to view him as a victim whose actions are justified. One egregious example of this is the John Wick movie franchise in which the protagonist slaughters hundreds of members of a criminal gang because one of them killed his puppy.

VICTIMS WHO VICTIMIZE

The truth is, the great evils of history are usually committed by those who believe they are victims. Today we look back upon the Nazis as the greatest monsters of history. Yet the Nazis convinced themselves and the German people that they were victims who needed to fight against those undermining and destroying their society.

Hitler's book *Mein Kampf* (my struggle) is a story of victimhood and injustice. In Hitler's view, Germans were treated unjustly by neighboring nations and by the Jews. The Jews had built a system that kept the German people down. The Jews manipulated world finances to keep the German people from rising up as rulers. The Jews weakened the German culture by spreading immorality and communism. Likewise, Germany was betrayed by other nations. After World War I, Germany's neighbors afflicted Germany with heavy reparations that weakened Germany to the point of collapse.

Even as the devil fed these feelings of unfairness and victimhood, he fed the pride of the German people. Hitler's story was soothing to their psyche. The Germans were actually a great race with god-like ancestors known as the Aryans. All their problems, defeats, and impoverishment were caused by their racial enemies. If they could reconnect to the glories of the German past, they would arise as rulers on the earth. The Germans were destined to rule other inferior races that had betrayed them and worked to keep them from achieving their full potential.

Upon this foundation of pride, victimhood, and bitterness, the German people mobilized against their oppressors. The world has rarely seen such a wave of hatred and murder as came from the heart of the German people. After the war, many Germans claimed they hadn't known what was going on but were also victims of the Nazis. This too is a lie. Research has shown that the unspeakable Nazi atrocities during World War II were not committed by a few extremist SS battalions but also by millions of ordinary German soldiers.

According to research by the United States Holocaust Memorial Museum, Nazi Germany and its allies established approximately forty-three thousand camps housing nearly twenty million inmates. These camps included thirty thousand slave labor camps, nine hundred eighty concentration camps, along with other camps specializing in forced abortion, euthanasia, sex slavery, and other horrors. Thousands of these camps were located in Germany itself. Practically every small town in Germany had a slave labor camp in its vicinity. Researchers concluded that there were so many slaves and camps within Germany it would have been nearly impossible for the average German not to know what was going on.

THE TACTICS OF SAUL ALINSKY

Jezebel's army is trained in the tactics of Saul Alinsky. Alinsky was a left-wing activist and community organizer who organized low-income communities in much the same way that trade union organizers organized workers. In 1971, Alinsky wrote his rulebook for activists, titled *Rules for Radicals*, and dedicated it to Lucifer himself.

Alinsky taught his followers to "organize" communities by identifying a community's grievances and stirring up resentment towards those blamed for causing those grievances until this agitation reached a boiling point. He also taught his followers how to personalize and polarize every conflict. Conflicts were not merely disagreements about issues but between good and evil. An enemy needed to be chosen and clearly identified as the source of all evil in the community.

This enemy was always a member of one of the evil "oppressor" groups who victimized the oppressed. The enemy might be one of the landlords, politicians, or business owners who were being blamed for the community's problems. Once clearly identified, the rage of the people could be mobilized against this enemy to force them to make the concessions demanded by the activists. Alinsky writes:

> *Keep the pressure on. Never let up . . . Ridicule is man's most potent weapon . . . Pick the target, freeze it, personalize it, and polarize it. Go after people and not institutions; people hurt faster than institutions.*

Alinsky taught his followers to stir up conflicts, then break all the rules in order to win those conflicts. He taught that in war the ends justify almost any means. False accusations and attacks against the enemy didn't need to be fair or even true. If you destroyed the enemy's life or reputation, so much the better. The important thing was to apply relentless pressure upon the target until the target complied and did what you wanted them to do.

OPPRESSIVE REPUBLICANS

Jezebel needs a controlling "statist" form of big government to build her system in America. In general, the Democratic Party has supported big government, including higher taxes and more government programs and handouts. The Democratic Party has thrown its full support behind a nationalized health care system (Obamacare), which is a form of socialized medicine. Most importantly, the Democratic Party has fully and completely embraced the "right" to abortion. These blood sacrifices to the god of self are an absolutely essential central component of the system that Jezebel is building.

In contrast, the Republican Party is supposedly in favor of a smaller government that abides by the limits placed upon it by the Constitution of the United States. Many Republican politicians are opposed to abortion rights. In reality of course, many Republican Party members have repeatedly voted for mind-boggling levels of deficit spending that makes big government possible. They have not taken effective action against legalized abortion. Their actions are only slightly less supportive of the massive, bloated, controlling federal bureaucracy than are the actions of the Democrats.

Nevertheless, the Republican Party has offered at least token resistance to Jezebel's plans. Therefore to Jezebel's army, they are the enemy. Jezebel's army uses Alinsky's tactics to attack those who believe in limited constitutional government. She paints these small-government conservatives as being heartless, greedy racists working to oppress minorities and other groups. She paints pro-life politicians as being motivated by hatred for women despite the fact that most pro-lifers are women.

JEZEBEL'S MINISTRY OF PROPAGANDA

It might seem strange that Jezebel is able to portray the party of Lincoln as being the racist oppressors of our nation and the party of the KKK as being its liberators. Jezebel is only able to pull this off with the use of the propaganda wing of her army, the mainstream media. In recent years, the national mainstream media apparatus has stopped even pretending to be a neutral dispenser of information as it throws its support completely behind left-wing politicians and politics.

This can be clearly seen in the "Russian Collusion" hoax that dominated America's airwaves for the first three and a half years of Donald Trump's presidency. For three years, the mainstream media breathlessly reported on the Trump campaign's supposed collusion with Russia. In the end, the truth came out. The Hillary Clinton campaign had paid some operatives to put together a file filled with lies and false accusations against Donald Trump known as the Steele Dossier. This file was leaked to the media and placed in the hands of the FBI who used it to launch their investigation. The entire "Russian Collusion" narrative was built upon this file.

The real collusionists were the Hillary Clinton campaign, federal investigators, and mainstream media, all of whom worked with paid Russian sources to create their case against Trump out of thin air. It was the dirtiest of dirty tricks empowered by a national media that has given up any resemblance of truthful, unbiased reporting. The whole corrupt project nearly succeeded in removing a lawfully elected sitting president.

If the media will use literally thousands of hours of airtime to support such lies, what else will they do? They have proven to be literally incapable of simply reporting the news in an evenhanded manner. Every story must fit the preplanned narrative, the storyline that best serves Jezebel's purposes.

OPPRESSIVE CHRISTIANS

Jezebel has manipulated many oppressed minorities into serving her purposes, channeling their rage towards her chosen targets. In recent years, a new wing of her army has taken the forefront, the LGBT activists. The new prominence of this movement is because her chosen target has shifted. Jezebel is no longer simply targeting the small-government conservatives who resisted her plans to build a controlling, suffocating government. She is now targeting biblical Christianity itself.

Who is the best group of activists to lead an attack against biblical Christianity? African Americans are predominantly confessing Christians. Many support big government, but they will not support a direct attack on Christianity. Likewise, a significant percentage of liberal women might support Jezebel's abortion agenda, but women do not form a unified political front that Jezebel can easily manipulate. A large percentage of American women are strongly pro-life and committed to their Christian faith. Many of America's most prominent conservative leaders are women.

LGBT activists are moving to the front lines of Jezebel's army because they have been taught that Bible-believing Christians are their enemy. The Bible clearly teaches that homosexual practice is sin. Jezebel uses this fact to teach gays, lesbians, and transgenders that Christians hate them, victimize them, and want to take away their rights. Jezebel teaches them that Christians are the oppressors and that they are the oppressed.

In fact, most conservative Christians are basically libertarian in their views on sexual issues. Most Bible-believing Christians don't want to see laws passed that would outlaw adultery or homosexual practices. Most Bible-believing Christians would agree that the government does not belong in our bedrooms, telling us what to do.

At the same time, conservative Bible-believing Christians believe homosexual practice is sinful and do not want to be a part of it. They don't want their children taught that homosexuality is a good thing. They don't want the government telling them what to teach in their churches and private Christian schools.

Most conservative Bible-believing Christians will gladly serve gays and lesbians in their businesses. They don't want to take away their civil rights, voting rights, or victimize them in any way whatsoever. But neither do they want to be forced to participate in gay weddings and other ceremonies they see as evil. They want to be left alone.

Jezebel does not tolerate religious liberty. Christians must be forced to celebrate homosexuality. Christian schools must hire gays and lesbians to teach their children. It's not enough for Christian owned businesses to serve gay customers. They must be forced to participate in gay weddings. If they don't, the power of the state will be used against them.

Jezebel tries to portray conservative Christians as the aggressors in the culture wars, working to bring America under a theocratic government. In fact, Jezebel is the aggressor and oppressor, working ceaselessly to stamp out religious freedom in our nation. She will not be satisfied until she has removed the worship of Yahweh from our land as she did in the land of Israel many years ago.

JEZEBEL'S ENDGAME

Jezebel is very, very skilled in this game. She has chosen her army and convinced them they are victims. She has chosen her enemy, conservative Christians. She portrays them to her army as moral monsters. She stirs up resentment and bitterness until her army is consumed with rage. She teaches her soldiers that they are not actually responsible for any of their own problems. She paints a picture of the glorious new society that will result if the hated oppressors are removed. And when the time is right, she unleashes her army of rage upon the earth. When this army marches, it feels that it is justified in all that it does even as it commits moral horrors.

Can you see this army rising in America? Do you think that Jezebel will raise up an army and not use it? She does not raise up an army without a purpose, without an end game in mind. As you see the rage of Jezebel's disciples building to a boiling point, know that she has chosen her targets and will use her army. The church in America will pass through persecution just as the true worshipers of Yahweh did in ancient Israel under Jezebel's rule.

Chapter Eleven

JEZEBEL'S LEADERS

As Jezebel builds her system, she needs the acquiescence of America's leaders. These leaders are not really part of Jezebel's army of rage, but they are not willing to stand up to Jezebel and her army. They are not the ones putting pressure on Jezebel's chosen targets. They are the targets of Jezebel's pressure. They include politicians, corporate leaders, and other men and women of position and influence in our society.

We can see the character and mentality of Jezebel's leaders in the men she manipulated in the story of Naboth (1 Kings 21). As we've already noted, Ahab surrendered his authority as a king to Jezebel. Using his signet ring, Jezebel was able to issue orders in Ahab's name to the elders of Naboth's hometown, instructing them to implement her plot to kill Naboth. In this example, we see the basic nature of Jezebel's leaders. These are weak men and women who refuse to stand in their God-given authority. When pressure is placed upon them, they give way to the pressure. They choose to obey Jezebel's commands rather than face her wrath.

BLACK LIVES MATTER AND CORPORATE AMERICA

In America today, it is remarkable to see how quickly and easily American leaders submit to Jezebel's authority. For example, the leaders of corporate

America practically fell over themselves trying to show how deeply committed they were to the Black Lives Matter movement. Under pressure from BLM activists, fifty of America's largest corporations pledged $49.5 billion to support the fight against racial inequality. Nearly all of America's major corporations publicly declared their support for the movement.

Black Lives Matter is led by Marxists and therefore works as an integral part of Jezebel's army. Evidence of this is found in a 2015 video where the co-founder of Black Lives Matter, Patrisse Cullors, declares that she and her fellow organizers are trained Marxists. They are trained in an ideology that literally seeks the destruction of corporate America.

The leaders of corporate America are some of the most powerful, wealthy, privileged, and connected people on this planet. They are driven, extremely hard-working men and women, always looking for the opportunity to dominate their corporate adversaries. They are not victims. They cannot pretend to be an oppressed class of people.

In Jezebel's moral hierarchy, it is the oppressed groups that are morally superior to the oppressors. The oppressors are the wealthy white elites, which is exactly what most of America's corporate leaders are. Why then do these corporate leaders support BLM?

Simply put, they fear the accusations and pressure of Jezebel's army. They know that if they don't give way to the pressure of these activist groups, they will be accused of being oppressors and racists. They want so desperately to show they are not oppressors that they will do almost anything to prove their allegiance to the system Jezebel is building. Faced with Jezebelic accusations of racism and sexism, they literally throw billions of dollars at the ones who are accusing them, immediately acquiescing to their accuser's demands They are willing to force their employees to undergo racial and LGBT sensitivity training in which they are given a crash course in critical theory.

One reason why America's leaders seem unwilling or unable to stand before Jezebel is that they have all been trained by Jezebel. America's political and corporate leaders, be they Democrat or Republican, have for the most part been trained in America's institutes of higher learning. In particular, America's top leaders in business, law, politics, medicine, and many other fields are likely to have passed through a very small number of America's top universities. Three of the last five presidents— George H.W. Bush, Bill Clinton and George W. Bush—attended Yale University. Obama and Trump attended other Ivy League schools.

Jezebel asserted her control over America's Ivy League universities a long time before she was able to assert it over the rest of American society. I attended an Ivy League university (Cornell University) in the early 1990s. Even then the Ivy League schools were dominated by political correctness, critical theory, and left-wing activism.

The point is that a very large percentage of America's top leaders are trained in schools controlled by the spirit of Jezebel. In those schools, they learn what kinds of views and opinions are acceptable and which are not. In those schools, they learn political correctness. They learn about the moral superiority of the oppressed and the moral depravity of the oppressors. They learn that traditional biblical views are simply not morally acceptable among the elites of American society. They learned to accept and celebrate sexual immorality. They learn the value system of Jezebel.

This training conditions America's top leaders to submit to the system Jezebel is building. When they are threatened with the accusations and character assassination of Jezebel's army, they quickly submit. They may be strong, aggressive men and women in one arena, but they are weak and submissive when it comes to Jezebel. Very few of America's business leaders and politicians are willing to face the venomous hatred and character assassination that Jezebel unleashes against anyone who tries to stand up to her.

In this way, America falls in line. Every major city in America holds parades and other events celebrating gay pride and sexual immorality. Politicians on both sides of the aisle are vocal in their support. Every American university does the same. Politicians from both parties embrace gay marriage as a civil right.

Everyone wants to be seen as tolerant and accepting of Jezebel's immorality and idolatrous religions. Everyone tolerates the intolerance of Jezebel and her minions. Nobody wants to speak out against sexual sin or the flood of New Age religion sweeping into the country. For Jezebel to succeed, she needs Ahab. She needs those in positions of authority who are willing to abdicate their responsibility and authority rather than stand up to her.

THE SIN OF EVE

Jezebel's nature can be seen as a maturing of the sin of Eve. In his book *The Valley*, Rick Joyner writes, "The spirit of Jezebel is the maturing of the evil that began when the first woman ate the fruit of the forbidden tree." Eve was created to walk alongside Adam, to help him and share in his responsibilities. The devil came to Eve and tempted her to eat the fruit of the tree of the knowledge of good and evil, thereby becoming "like God."

In the story of Eve (Genesis 3), we see Eve's dissatisfaction with all that God had given her. In the midst of such blessing, she felt cheated. She felt God was withholding something good from her. She looked at the beautiful fruit of the tree of the knowledge of good and evil and felt tempted to take what was not given to her. To eat the fruit that was forbidden to her so she could receive a kind of wisdom. So she could be like God. Taking the fruit, she ate it and gave it to her husband to eat as well.

Perhaps the besetting sins of men and women are somewhat different, although they also overlap to a large degree. In the case of Eve, we see her deep dissatisfaction with what God has given her. It may be that Jezebel is skilled in manipulating this dissatisfaction in women, convincing women that if they lay down their lives to nurture and serve their children and husbands, they will be cheated. She teaches a woman to use seduction, manipulation, and even witchcraft to get what she wants from a man who is physically stronger than her. She enables a woman to force her will upon others.

THE SIN OF ADAM

And it may be that in the same story we can see one of the primary besetting sins of a man. Adam was given responsibility to tend the garden before Eve even existed. Before Eve even existed, the Lord spoke to Adam:

> *Of every tree of the garden you may freely eat; but of the tree of the knowledge of good and evil you shall not eat, for in the day that you eat of it you shall surely die. (Genesis 2:16-17 NKJV)*

Yet Adam surrendered his God-given responsibility and authority and obeyed his wife instead of God. When confronted by God, he blamed his wife and his Creator for his sin.

> *The woman whom You gave to be with me, she gave me of the tree, and I ate. (Genesis 3:12 NKJV)*

Just as dissatisfaction may be one of the besetting sins of women, this refusal to lead and take responsibility may be one of the besetting sins of men. Instead of seeking to know and obey the voice of the Lord, such a man gives way to pressure and tries to keep the people around him happy.

To truly take up one's responsibilities and authority is costly. Adam was given dominion over all the beasts of the earth, but he was also given the garden to tend and to keep. He was given work to do. The weight of responsibility, authority, and the hard work that goes with it is heavy. And after the fall of humankind, it became much heavier.

> *Then to Adam He [God] said, "Because you have heeded the voice of your wife, and have eaten from the tree of which I commanded you, saying, 'You shall not eat of it': cursed is the ground for your sake; in toil you shall eat of it all the days of your life. Both thorns and thistles it shall bring forth for you, and you shall eat the herb of the field. In the sweat of your face you shall eat bread till you return to the ground, for*

out of it you were taken; for dust you are, and to dust you shall return. (Genesis 3:17-19 NKJV)

A weak man is tempted to shirk his responsibilities, to let someone else carry the burden, so that he can spend his life living for himself and his appetites. It is much easier for a man to shirk his God-given responsibilities and authority than it is for him to carry them.

In contrast, a strong man carries the weight of responsibility for himself and his family. He is willing to work long hours without complaint. He places the needs of others ahead of his own. A strong man knows what he is fighting for and is willing to lay everything down and pay any price to stand for what is right.

A strong man is faithful. He is there when you need him. He isn't a cheater, liar, or moocher. His character goes deep, and he won't change his moral standards to please you.

A strong man is strong when the people around him need him to be strong. When crisis comes, he isn't quivering with fear in a corner. He takes the action that needs to be taken whatever the personal cost.

A strong man gives security to all who are around him. When enemies threaten those under his authority, he is willing to risk his life to confront them. He provides a safe place for his children to grow and flourish. His love and protection enables his daughters to become strong women, his sons to become strong men.

A strong man doesn't allow Jezebel to push him aside in any area of authority. He doesn't allow Jezebel to bring her lies into schools, churches, or the home. He doesn't relinquish his authority just because Jezebel accuses him and tells him that he is part of an evil patriarchy.

A strong and godly man is not controlled by his appetites. He refuses to engage in sexual activity outside of the covenant of marriage. He walks in holy covenant with his God and with his wife. He would rather die than break the covenant with his God or his marriage partner.

Jezebel hates strong and godly men. Jezebel needs men who will easily lie and break covenant, easily be swayed by the pressures of life and by their own evil desires. Such men she can manipulate and control.

WEAK MEN

Weak men live for themselves and their appetites. If a weak man holds a position of authority, he uses it to serve himself and satisfy his appetite for money, glory, and sexual conquest. He has no higher purpose, no higher goal, than to satisfy the demands of his flesh.

Some weak man feel they can satisfy their desires in life without having a position of authority or responsibility. There are many lazy men who work as little as possible and use the little money they make on themselves. Much of their energy is spent on self-gratification. They amuse themselves with hobbies, video games, pornography, and addictions. They engage in sexual relationships without commitment or taking responsibility for anyone else's welfare. They live for themselves with no higher purpose in life.

Weak men are controlled by their appetites and by Jezebel. She preys upon her victim's weaknesses, promising she will get him what he wants while bringing him into covenants and agreements with hell. A man might feel, for instance, rejected and mistreated by the women in his life. It is so easy to make an alliance with Jezebel to feed his lust and desire without the cost and responsibilities of a lifelong marriage covenant. It is so easy to sit down with a laptop computer and a pornographic video. There is no cost, no relationship, no strings attached. Simply a man and his desires.

Weak men are susceptible to Jezebel's seduction and end up compromising with some form of sexual immorality. A weak man might not literally commit adultery with another woman but he will engage in other forms of immoral behavior such as masturbation and pornography. If confronted, he pleads the weakness of his flesh and declares that all men struggle as he does.

In reality, when a man obeys a spirit of lust and masturbates to perverse images, covenantal connections are formed. As time goes on, he might claim to be addicted to pornography. In reality, he has come under a kind of spiritual bondage, a covenantal connection to spirits of lust. This bondage leads him down a dark path. Images of pretty women that used to excite him are no longer interesting to him. He searches out increasingly perverse and degrading forms of pornography as he enters a kind of spiritual slavery.

The battle with Jezebel is primarily a spiritual battle. Can men who are addicted to pornography in their private lives take a stand against Jezebel's forces? Can such a man stand against Jezebel when she wants to teach young children about oral and anal sex in school? Can such a man call a church youth group to live lives of sexual purity?

A man who is addicted to pornography can certainly say the right words, but his words will not carry the convicting power of the Holy Spirit. In reality, he has given away his spiritual authority, and he has nothing positive to bring to the struggle against Jezebel.

Many of America's influential male leaders have deeply compromised with Jezebel in their personal lives and come under her control. How many of America's top politicians and corporate leaders visited the island owned by the convicted pedophile Jeffrey Epstein? How many flew on his private jet, nicknamed the "Lolita Express", where orgies with under-aged girls were known to take place? Bill Gates and Bill Clinton and were among those who were friends of Mr. Epstein. Bill Clinton flew on the Lolita Express twenty-six times.

It seems that Jeffrey Epstein may have kept video evidence of the sexual escapades of his visitors. The New Zealand Herald reports: "Insiders have claimed that Epstein used the cameras to record his 'guests' raping under-aged girls, using the tapes to blackmail them."

In this way, Jezebel gains control over key leaders. They become part of the network of political and economic leaders that are fully under her control just as she controlled the elders of Israel. They are afraid to speak out against anything that she does because she can destroy them.

Weak men are fearful men, susceptible to the intimidation of Jezebel. Weak men value their social standing and their positions in church, business, and community more than they care about Jezebel's victims. Jezebel targets this cowardice, threatening such a man with loss of his position of authority and with character assassination. The fearful man quickly complies with her demands.

America has many such Ahabs. They are men who seem to carry great authority and influence in our nation. They seem to be strong men, but they have actually come under the control of Jezebel, who controls and manipulates them completely. Such men never stand firm when the test comes. They always compromise under pressure, allowing Jezebel to get what she wants.

Chapter Twelve

THE AMERICAN FAMILY AND JEZEBEL

The nuclear family is the foundation of American society. If the family breaks down, it will ultimately lead to the breakdown of the nation. Jezebel understands the foundational role of the nuclear family, and she works ceaselessly to weaken, undermine, and ultimately destroy it so that she can construct her new system.

To destroy the family, Jezebel works to remove fathers from the home. A father provides protection, provision, love, and discipline. When the biological father is removed from a household, an enormous vacuum is created. Jezebel is there to fill in the vacuum with the pretense of meeting the emotional and financial needs of the mother and the children.

In this chapter, we will look at the removal of fathers and its effects on the American family. I will focus more on fathers than mothers in this chapter, not because fathers are more important, but because their role in the American family has come under such sustained attack.

THE BREAKDOWN OF THE AFRICAN-AMERICAN FAMILY

Consider the breakdown of the African-American family that has taken place during the past seventy years and the repercussions of that breakdown. If we look at what has taken place, we can see Jezebel's playbook for destroying all American families and our society in general.

The African-American community passed through almost unimaginable hardship and suffering in their American experience. Yet in the midst of these hardships, the African-American family survived. Even during the days of slavery when marriage between slaves was illegal, most African-American children grew up in the same house as their biological mother and father.[1] Up till about 1950, a slightly higher percentage of black adults were married than white adults. In 1950, just nine percent of black children lived without their father.[2]

Today, nearly seventy percent of African-American children grow up in a home without the presence of their biological father. This disintegration of the African-American nuclear family took place during the late 1960s and early 1970s, during which time the percentage of African-America homes led by a single parent increased from thirty percent to more than fifty percent. Since that time, the rate has increased to about seventy percent, where it has remained.

What took place in the 1960s that could be responsible for such an increase in single parent homes? In 1964, Lyndon Johnson launched the war on poverty. Dozens of "Great Society" social welfare programs were initiated with the purpose of reducing poverty. About the same time, the sexual revolution began.

The Great Society social welfare programs were very generous. In 1975, researchers estimated that a single mother would need a job earning more than twenty thousand dollars per year to match what government programs would give her for sitting at home.[3] Twenty thousand dollars in 1975 is the equivalent of over a hundred thousand today.

Even worse, these generous government benefits were structured in such a way that marriage was penalized. Paul E. Peterson, professor of government at Harvard University, writes:

---

[1] The Black Family in Slavery and Freedom, 1750–1925, by Herbert Gutman
[2] An Alternative Black History Month by Jason L. Riley
[3] Government Should Subsidize, Not Tax, Marriage by Paul E. Peterson

Some programs actively discouraged marriage… Welfare assistance went to mothers so long as no male was boarding in the household. Marriage to an employed male, even one earning the minimum wage, placed at risk a mother's economic well-being.

THE SEXUAL REVOLUTION

The second factor that worked against African-American families was the sexual revolution, a social movement that began in the early 1960s in America and other developed nations and lasted through the 1980s. In this revolution, people experienced "sexual liberation" from traditional moral values. The widespread use of contraception and legalization of abortion helped make the revolution possible. A broad range of sexual behaviors, including premarital sex, extramarital sex, homosexuality, masturbation, and pornography, became acceptable in American society as the revolution ran its course.

The sexual revolution taught our nation that sexual intercourse is merely a pleasurable activity that can be indulged in without any serious consequences, without the formation of a covenant or any commitment between the two parties. In reality, there is no such thing as consequence-free sex. Sex always involves a connection between two people. From the beginning, God made it this way that two shall be joined and become one (Genesis 2:24). When sexual intercourse takes place and the two parties then go their own way, there is the pain of a broken connection. Something meant to be for life has been torn apart.

Women who engage in promiscuity often seem to feel this pain more acutely than men. They feel like something has been stolen from them. They often become embittered against the men who "use" them even if they have willingly engaged in sexual activities with them.

It turns out that premarital sexual intercourse weakens the institution of marriage. The National Survey of Family Growth carried out surveys that measured the relationship between divorce and the number of sexual partners women had prior to marriage. A survey conducted between 2011-2013 revealed that women who married as virgins had approximately a six percent chance of experiencing a divorce within the first five years of marriage. In contrast, women who had more than ten sexual partners prior to marriage experienced a divorce rate of thirty-three percent in their first five years of marriage. In other words, divorce rates were about six times higher in the first five years of marriage for women who had many sexual partners prior to marriage compared to virgins.

The sexual revolution weakened Americans' commitment to marriage in other ways. As the revolution progressed, cohabitation was no longer frowned upon by American society, causing millions of American couples to no longer fully commit themselves to their partners. It became acceptable for a couple to simply live together for as long as it was convenient to do so before moving on to someone else. Unfortunately, cohabitation does not provide the same long-term family stability as traditional marriage.

What do you think happened? Generous government programs made single motherhood possible, sometimes even profitable. The sexual revolution weakened the institution of marriage. It no longer seemed morally necessary or financially beneficial for a couple to marry.

The combination of these two factors had an outsized effect on the African-American community, causing the marriage rate in African-American communities to begin its precipitous decline. Two generations of African-American children have been raised in homes without the presence of their fathers. The results have been disastrous. In his article "The Legacy of the Welfare State," Walter Williams writes:

> *The number one problem among blacks is the effects stemming from a very weak family structure. Children from fatherless homes are likelier to drop out of high school, die by suicide, have behavioral disorders, join gangs, commit crimes, and end up in prison. They are also likelier to live in poverty-stricken households.*

The same forces that affected African-American families are affecting families of all races with somewhat delayed effects. If you study any lower-income white community in America today in which a large percentage of the people have become dependent on social welfare programs, you will likely find the same breakdown of the family and the same ensuing consequences that can be found in the African-American community.

In America as a whole, marriage rates have declined so that only fifty percent of adults from the ages of 18-44 have ever been married. Only three in five children under the age of eighteen live with both biological parents in America today.

JEZEBEL AND DIVORCE

Michael Rosenfeld, a sociologist from Stanford University, analyzed data from representative surveys of two thousand American heterosexual adults taken between 2009 to 2015. He concluded that forty-two to forty-five percent of first marriages end in divorce, sixty percent of second marriages, and seventy-three percent of third marriages.

Rosenfeld also noted that most of these divorces are being filed by women. Approximately seventy percent of divorces in the United States are filed by women. For the most part, these divorces are not being filed because of abuse or even adultery on the part of the man. Most are being filed simply because the woman feels dissatisfied with her marriage and is seeking greater personal happiness. Yet in this search for happiness and personal fulfillment, lives are destroyed.

A woman controlled by Jezebel is likely to despise her husband and to strive for someone better. The man who marries a woman under the control of Jezebel will discover that she will leave him for someone of higher status when it suits her interests. On the way out, she will do everything in her power to destroy him emotionally and financially. The American legal system will likely support her in doing this.

An American woman under the influence of Jezebel can engage in serial extramarital affairs, and her husband can do nothing about it. She can file a no-fault divorce claim and take the children for herself. If he is lucky, he will be able to visit with them on weekends. She can take half of the family assets, and he will need to pay her monthly support, sometimes for the rest of her life. If he refuses, he will be thrown in jail.

This is the system of no-fault divorce that is prevalent in America today. It is far too easy to get divorced in America today. It is far too easy for a woman to destroy the lives of her husband and her children for no reason at all apart from her own dissatisfaction, the feeling that she deserves better than what her husband can offer.

Of course, many women are the victims of abusive men. It is likely that most readers know of men who have been abusive and unfaithful towards their wives. Most of us know of divorces that needed to take place because of the evil behavior of the men involved. Nevertheless, the numbers indicate that this is not the primary cause of divorce in America today.

THE AUTHORITY OF A FATHER

Jezebel's destruction of the American family has focused on the removal of fathers and their authority from the home. One of Jezebel's central deceptions in our nation today is that a man who walks in authority always does so for selfish purposes. Jezebel portrays men, especially white men, as oppressors unless they fully embrace her agenda. He is part of a patriarchal system that works to keep women down. He uses his authority and position for his own benefit, not the benefit of others. This message is drilled home in classrooms across America.

The biblical view of authority is very different. True godly authority always carries a high price. Jesus has the highest authority, and He paid the highest price. The apostle Paul wrote:

> *Wives, submit to your own husbands, as is fitting in the Lord.* (Colossians 3:18 NKJV)

> *Husbands, love your wives, just as Christ also loved the church and gave Himself for her. (Ephesians 5:25 NKJV)*

When Paul writes about the authority of the husband in the marriage relationship, he also writes about the cost of that authority. How did Christ love the church? He gave everything He had, including His own life, for His bride. Quite simply, a man is supposed to lead in the marriage relationship in a sacrificial way, making every decision out of love for his bride and his family, putting their interests ahead of his own. This is the very essence of strong godly authority.

God gives a man strength and authority to serve others, not to serve himself. A man is called to use that strength and authority to serve and protect those who are weaker. This authority provides security and protection for those who are under it.

MOTHERS

In Jezebel's system, the mother is the real head of the household, and the government recognizes and supports her authority. This can be seen in the case of divorce, in which the government usually awards custody of the children to the mother.

Fathers cannot be removed from a family without causing widespread repercussions. The task of nurturing a child is so overwhelming, so consuming, that it takes more than one person. A mother needs a husband who protects and provides for the family as she focuses her attention on the needs of the child.

When a man isn't present to provide for and protect a household, mothers and children look elsewhere. Inevitably, they turn to the government for help. The government offers programs that enable a woman to raise her children without the help of the father. The government takes the place of the father, offering the support that makes it possible for a family to survive. The mother frequently becomes dependent on government programs. She repays the government with her vote, usually voting for those who promise bigger government, more programs, and handouts. Married women, on the other hand, are more likely to vote for smaller government and politically conservative policies.

As the family breaks down, mothers demand more help from the government. As dependency on the government increases, the role of fathers is diminished all the more. Mothers and children grow up completely dependent upon the welfare state, completely dependent upon a system controlled by Jezebel.

FATHERS AND THE PLAYBOY MENTALITY

Just as government intervention makes it possible for women to be single mothers, it also takes away the need for men to be fathers. Men need a cause, something to give their lives for. Young men compete with each other to join elite military units where they can give all that they have for their country. Men have a strong desire to be a hero and provider for their families.

It has been noted by many experts on marriage that women need love and men need respect. One of the worst things a man can say to his wife is "I respect you, but I don't love you." One of the worst things a wife can say to her husband is "I love you, but I don't respect you." This may be why the Bible says:

> However, each one of you also must love his wife as he loves himself, and the wife must respect her husband. (Ephesians 5:33 NIV)

This doesn't mean that a woman doesn't need to be respected or that a man doesn't need to be loved. It just means their emotional priorities are somewhat different.

Jezebel understands how a man is wired. She knows that if a man is dishonored enough, it kills something inside of him. Instead of acting honorably and giving his life to provide for and to serve his family, he will feel like just giving up and living for himself and his appetites.

Fathers have been consistently dishonored by popular culture in America. If you watch a hundred television shows in America, you will see a pattern in the families depicted. The father is the butt of jokes, the buffoon, the fool. He might be cruel and abusive. He is Al Bundy, Homer Simpson, Stan Smith. If the show offers a voice of wisdom or morality, it is voiced by the mother or children.

The man who is honored in Hollywood is usually the playboy, the one who can convince beautiful women to get in bed with him. He is not usually the man who commits himself to one woman for a lifetime, the man who works a steady job to provide for his family. He is not the one who leads his family in the ways of the Lord with love and discipline.

A father is no longer permitted to physically discipline his children in much of America. Our society no longer recognizes the distinction between child abuse and appropriate physical discipline. Our society doesn't recognize the fact that discipline done with love and consistency is of great benefit to every child, as Scripture states:

> *He who spares his rod hates his son, But he who loves him disciplines him promptly. (Proverbs 13:24 NKJV)*

Parents who do not use physical discipline are likely to become so frustrated with their child that they say things they later regret. Which will have a greater negative long-term effect on a child: words spoken in anger and frustration about the child or a restrained paddling? Negative words spoken by a parent will stick to a child for a lifetime. The paddling stings for a few seconds at most.

Physical discipline must obviously be done with much restraint, and it must be done with love instead of anger. If you are angry with your child, don't use physical discipline at that moment. Wait a while so that you don't overreact to what has happened. And when the physical discipline is over, hold your child and let them know that they are loved.

An honorable man can't just sit and watch his wife and children starve to death. He will do what is necessary to provide for them. Even a less than honorable man will feel compelled to do what is necessary to provide for his own offspring.

But what if it isn't necessary to provide for one's offspring? What if a man knows that the government will provide for his offspring, that they aren't in danger of suffering if he does nothing? Or even worse, what if he knows that his financial contribution to his family will actually harm their welfare, disqualifying them from government assistance?

What if a man receives no respect in his own household? What if his own children treat him with contempt and he doesn't feel he can discipline them in any meaningful way? What if there is no sense of gratefulness for all the hours he spends working to provide for them?

These realities give the less than honorable man a way out. Why work so hard to provide for one's offspring? Why not live for oneself? Why commit your life to one woman when there are so many others out there? Why not play the field and have sex with as many women as possible?

In this way, men submit to Jezebel's plans. Instead of giving themselves to one woman and working to build a strong family, they become aimless and lost. They carry no responsibility or authority. They become weak and selfish men that nobody can depend upon.

YOUNG WOMEN

The loss of a father hits young women particularly hard. A father provides a father's love that only a father can give. Young women who grow up without this love and acceptance feel this loss and look for it elsewhere. Typically, they search for it in relationships with young men as they try to find what is missing in their lives. Young women who grow up in single-parent homes engage in sexual intercourse at a younger age with more sexual partners than those who grow up in two-parent homes.

Many young men learn how to exploit and manipulate the emotional vulnerability of young women. A young man learns to tell a young woman what she wants to hear so that she will give him what he wants. Once his conquest has succeeded, he drops her and moves on to the next. Meanwhile, the young woman is left with a broken heart and vulnerable for the next young man and his promises.

Young teenage girls need the protection of a father. A father doesn't have romanticized notions about the motives of young men. He understands young men quite a bit better than does a teenage girl. A loving father places limits on his daughter's social life for her own good. He doesn't just let her date the first drug dealer who is attracted to her. He confronts the wolves, the players who just want to add her to their list of sexual conquests.

Over time, a fatherless young woman has her heart repeatedly wounded in relationships with young men. These wounds eventually harden, and the young woman decides to no longer give her heart to a man. When she enters a relationship with a man, she is distrustful and turns against him when her feelings of rejection and abandonment are triggered. She might decide that men are basically scum who can't be trusted. They provide some companionship and sexual stimulation but not much more. Such a woman becomes vulnerable to Jezebel, who uses wounded and angry women in her army.

The woman who was raised by a single mother is more likely to become a single mother herself. If her mother was dependent on government programs, she is also likely to live her life in dependency. Men come and go, but the government is always there.

SONS AND THE LACK OF A FATHER

Young men need fathers. They need a father's love and discipline. They need someone to look up to, someone who can teach them how to live their lives. Young men instinctively look for these mentors. A strong and capable father is the best person to provide this for a young man.

A mother nurtures her son. A father brings a somewhat different perspective. He understands that young men (and women) need challenges. They need to be pushed to their limit so that they become strong and able to face the challenges of life.

If the father is missing from the house, a young man will look for what the father provides elsewhere. Many young men are drawn towards military life with its strict discipline, clear lines of authority, and physical challenges. Some search for authority and mentorship in more negative ways.

If you study the makeup of criminal gangs, you are likely to discover that nearly all of the young men involved did not grow up with fathers. Young men crave the sense of belonging that is provided by a gang. They admire the gang leaders, who seem to be tougher than everyone else. They accept the authority of the gang leaders and the discipline they provide, no matter how cruel that discipline might be.

The point is that young people crave authority, discipline, and structure. A vacuum of authority and discipline does not last for long. The young woman who either rebels against the authority of her parents or is rejected by her parents is likely to end up under the "authority" of an abusive boyfriend. The young man who rejects the authority of his parents might end up being disciplined by the state.

My father works as a prison psychiatrist. He tells me that when he counsels prisoners, he asks them about their relationship with their mother, not their father. He doesn't bother asking them about their father because none of them have a father. They grew up with the love and nurture of a mother but not with the love and discipline provided by a father. They became undisciplined and lawless, and the prison system ended up providing the discipline that was lacking in their lives.

BANKRUPTING THE NATION

It is difficult to calculate the cost of a broken family. Apart from the ruined lives, broken families are expensive. How many people suffering from mental illnesses come from broken homes, and how much does it cost to treat them? How much does it cost the prison system to house a prisoner from a broken home? How much does it cost to support one fatherless family that has become financially dependent on the government? How many trillions of dollars do the social welfare programs such as Medicaid cost?

I am not going to try to calculate these costs except to say the financial costs of family breakdowns are enormous. Intact families prosper, pay taxes, and increase the financial stability of a nation. Individuals from broken families are far more likely to become dependent on the government at a high cost to everyone.

As the American family has broken down, the American economy is headed off a cliff. In 2021, the federal budget was $6.818 trillion. The federal budget deficit was $2.77 trillion. The federal debt is approaching $28 trillion. These numbers are astronomical and unsustainable. It doesn't take an economist to know that America is bankrupt and that our years of prosperity are coming to an end.

Of course, Jezebel needs the present system to collapse so that she can build a system in which the government supports and enforces the worship of the idol of self. Removing fathers from their God-given position makes the implementation of Jezebel's plans possible. When fathers are removed, men become selfish creatures driven by their appetites, bound in sexual immorality, and unable or unwilling to stand in their authority and resist her control. Women become emotionally wounded, bound by sexual immorality, dependent upon the government, and vulnerable to Jezebel's manipulation. And Jezebel is ready to step into every vacuum of responsibility and authority that she has worked to create.

Chapter Thirteen

THE NOBLE WOMEN AND JEZEBEL

Proverbs 31:10-31 describes a woman who is strong and noble, a woman who fears God, a woman who brings blessing to everyone around her. This noble woman is the antithesis to Jezebel and everything she stands for. During the last days of this age, this woman will be used by God to expose the deceptions of Jezebel as she reveals the true dignity and beauty of womanhood.

In this chapter, we will briefly study this noble woman. Women who understand what God has called them to be are less susceptible to the lies of Jezebel. Women who become what God has called them to be will destroy Jezebel's plans to rule this earth.

A STRONG WOMAN

The noble woman of Proverbs 31 is a strong and loving woman. Verse 17 reads, "She girds herself with strength, and strengthens her arms." Verse 25 reads, "Strength and honor are her clothing; she shall rejoice in time to come."

The strength of the noble woman is different from the strength of Jezebel. Jezebel uses a kind of strength as she tries to dominate everyone in her life through control and manipulation. The strength of the noble woman is not used to dominate others but rather to serve them and build them up.

The strength of the noble woman is seen in those she builds up around her—her husband, children, and community. This woman works hard, rising early and going to bed late. Early in the morning before sunrise, she prepares food for her family and for the family's workers. She works with wool and flax, spinning and weaving them to create cloth for the garments that clothe her family. Everyone in her household is well cared for.

Even the poor of the city are blessed by the work of this woman. Verse 20 says, "She extends her hand to the poor, Yes, she reaches out her hands to the needy."

MARRIAGE

Jezebel teaches women to use and control weak men and to despise and destroy men who walk in godly authority. She never teaches a woman how to sacrificially love and serve a man. The thought of working hard to serve one's husband and family goes against everything Jezebel stands for. Jezebel teaches women to control and use men, not to become one with a man.

In the noble woman, we see a loving and trusting relationship between her and her husband. The noble woman understands that the welfare of her husband and family are closely connected to her own welfare, as God told Adam just before He created Eve.

> And the LORD God said, "It is not good that man should be alone; I will make him a helper comparable to him." (Genesis 2:18 NKJV)

It isn't in independence that the strength of this woman is seen. Eve was created as a helpmeet, a companion for Adam. The noble woman understands that this intimate connection with a man is part of what she was created for. Together, they build a family. Together, they love and serve one another. When she works for the welfare of her husband, she is promoting her own welfare, prosperity, and success. In the same passage, we see the response of her husband to such a woman.

> *The heart of her husband safely trusts her; so he will have no lack of gain. She does him good and not evil all the days of her life. (Proverbs 31:11-12 NKJV)*

The noble wife is wise and good. Verse 26 says, "She opens her mouth with wisdom, and on her tongue is the law of kindness." The husband knows the wisdom of his wife and her good heart. He knows that every resource placed in her hands will be used wisely. Therefore, he trusts her in every part of life.

A BUSINESSWOMAN

The noble woman of Proverbs is a businesswoman. She is successful and prosperous. She buys and sells merchandise (v. 18). She invests in real estate and buys a field, then uses the profits from her business endeavors to plant a vineyard in the field she purchased (v. 16).

This passage concludes in verse 31, "Give her of the fruit of her hands." What this means is that this businesswoman was financially autonomous, keeping and investing her profits. While most women when this scripture was written were financially dependent upon their husbands, the noble woman in this passage was free to make her own financial decisions.

This freedom didn't come because she stood up for herself and rebelled against her husband's authority, but because her husband trusted her completely. The husband of a noble woman knows he doesn't need to keep an eye on what she is doing with her investments. He knows that she is using her money and investments for the good of himself and the entire household. He knows that she works for his good and not his harm all the days of her life.

MOTHERHOOD

The noble woman is a mother who loves, nurtures, and serves her children. Motherhood is a high calling, the source of life itself. It is inseparable from the feminine nature, from God's plan and purpose for woman. In motherhood, a woman gives everything she has for the sake of another.

The modern feminist movement has succeeded in convincing many women that children and husbands are an obstacle to their own happiness and fulfillment in life. Many women are convinced that their own happiness should take priority over their children's welfare. Many divorce their husbands despite the great suffering and confusion a divorce causes for the children. Even worse, feminists have convinced many women that their most important right is their right to kill their own child.

What could be more destructive than to turn a woman against motherhood itself? What could be more destructive than to turn a woman against her own child, murdering it so that she can be free to live the life she wants? Is there any sin that can turn a woman so completely from God's intentions? For a woman to reject the call to care and nurture her own offspring to the extent that she kills that offspring is a complete rejection of God's plan and purpose, an embrace of a deep evil. This is the work of Jezebel, who brought the industrial-scale child sacrifices of the Phoenicians into the land of Israel.

WORKING WITH WHAT SHE HAS

Jezebel works to turn women into selfish, controlling, dissatisfied creatures who are a destructive force in the lives of everyone around them. Jezebel teaches a woman to despise what is given to her in life.

In contrast, the noble woman works with what she has rather than striving to take what she doesn't have. She values what she has been given in life and works to see it prosper. She loves, values, and honors her husband and works to help him succeed in life. She loves and values her children and does all she can for them. She values her business, and it multiplies. Her husband is a respected elder of the city (v. 23), at least in part because of the way she has worked to support him in their life together. Every part of her life is fruitful and blessed like a well-tended garden.

This desire to love, nurture, and serve one's family is so strong in a godly woman that many will even drop out of high-pressure careers so they can dedicate their time to raising a family. Others work parttime for the same reason. They give up income, prestige, and position as they do so.

Feminists have frequently despised stay-at-home moms, seeing them as enablers of the patriarchy. Some term them breeders and worse because of the way such moms prioritize the needs of their families above themselves. They despise the choice and sacrifice these women make. They think women should focus their lives on rising to the top in their careers, working to displace the men representing the patriarchy.

I am not in favor of any kind of glass ceiling or limitations of any kind for women in the workplace. The woman who chooses to focus her life on having a successful career should be free to do so. If there are unnecessary barriers that can be removed to help women succeed in the workplace, they should be removed. If there are company policies that hinder women from working their way to the top of a company, they should be changed. Strong and capable women can certainly succeed in every field, and any policies that favor men over women should be changed.

Nevertheless, we should recognize that God has put something very special in women that should be honored. When a woman chooses to place a greater priority on her family than her career, we should honor that choice. When a woman chooses to prioritize the needs of her family over her own career, she should be free to do so without feeling condemned. Women who choose to put their families ahead of themselves should be honored, not despised. They are making a noble sacrifice.

PRAISE AND HONOR

Jezebel seeks to exalt herself, to raise herself above everyone around her. The noble woman does the opposite, humbling herself and serving those around her. Yet even as she humbles herself, she receives much honor from the ones that she has served, as we see in the final verses of this passage.

Her children rise up and call her blessed; Her husband also, and he praises her: "Many daughters have done well, but you excel them all." Charm is deceitful and beauty is passing, but a woman who fears the LORD, she shall be praised. Give her of the fruit of her hands, and let her own works praise her in the gates. (Proverbs 31:28-31 NKJV)

The noble woman's own husband and children "rise up and call her blessed." Her husband praises her, telling her that she excels more than all other women. Even in the city gates, the elders of the city talk about the accomplishments of this woman. She doesn't seek to be honored, but she ends up receiving much honor.

If Jezebel represents the fullness of the sin of Eve, the noble woman represents the bride of Christ. In the last days, evil will come to maturity. Jezebel will seek to exalt herself and her idols in the nations of the earth. Women who embrace her ways will demonstrate great selfishness and evil.

And in every nation, the bride of Christ will shine. Women will arise who love the Lord with all their heart, soul, mind, and strength. They will love wholeheartedly the family and other people God places in their life. They will be very fruitful in their lives, businesses, and ministries. They will do great works, and they will be honored for eternity.

Chapter Fourteen

JEZEBEL'S CHURCHES

One of the ultimate goals of Jezebel is to bring her idolatry right into the temple, to replace the worship of Yahweh with the worship of idols. Today, Jezebel is working to establish the idolatry of self inside the church, inside the temple of God. Some churches have fully embraced this idolatry of self as they permit the spirit of Jezebel to minister freely in their churches.

EASTLAKE COMMUNITY CHURCH

Consider the example of Ryan Meeks, former lead pastor of the Seattle-area Eastlake Community Church, which at one time was one of the fastest growing evangelical megachurches in America. Like most evangelical churches, ECC faced the question of how to handle the issue of homosexuality. Should practicing homosexuals be welcomed as full members in the church? Should the church recognize and support gay marriage?

Biblically, the answer to this question is clear. Homosexual practice is condemned in both the Old and New Testament. Scriptures that condemn homosexual practice include Leviticus 18:22, 20:13; Romans 1:18-32; 1 Corinthians 6:9-11; 1 Timothy 1:8-10; and Jude 7. These scriptures are unequivocal in their condemnation of homosexual practice.

But just as the devil approached Eve with the words "Did God really say, 'You shall not eat of every tree of the garden?'", Jezebel teaches that in fact God does not condemn homosexuality in scripture. The scriptures which seem to be condemning homosexuality are actually only condemning the cultic male prostitution that took place in the temples of Baal. Or they are speaking about people driven by lust as they engage in sexual activity with each other. They are not speaking about two homosexuals living in a committed, loving relationship with each other.

With this kind of logic, the clear meaning of Scripture is pushed aside. Churches are pressured to accept the idolatrous moral standards of modern American society. Our society has decided that every form of sexual perversion is good, therefore it is good and must be celebrated.

Ryan Meeks and ECC accepted this kind of logic and eventually took the step of publicly embracing homosexuality. On January 25, 2015, the church publicly accepted LGBT persons into full membership. At the LGBT affirmation ceremony, Meeks stated:

> *I cannot bear to move forward in my life as a part of a faith community where my friends are not welcome to both serve and receive communion, to have equal welcome into the community of Christianity, of following Jesus. From this point forward, we're going to keep doing what we've always done, as we aim for Jesus.*

With these words, Ryan welcomed into church membership those engaged in open homosexual relationships and claimed that Jesus was the one leading him to do so. This is the work of Jezebel, in which the church conforms to the idolatrous value system of the surrounding society instead of actually making disciples of Jesus Christ. Jesus stated forthrightly:

> *You are the salt of the earth; but if the salt loses its flavor, how shall it be seasoned? It is then good for nothing but to be thrown out and trampled underfoot by men. (Matthew 5:13 NKJV)*

A church that loses its love for biblical truth and conforms to the lies of the surrounding society becomes useless for the kingdom of heaven. It becomes part of the world's system and loses its transforming power. Ryan himself recognized that once ECC made the choice to reject the clear meaning of Scripture and embrace homosexuality, the church started sliding down a slippery slope. He described the evolution of ECC in this way.

> *At one point you could have called us a tiny fledgling church plant, and then we were a purpose-driven "Health Award" winner in 2006, and then we were one of Outreach Magazine's fastest-growing churches in America and we were a multi-site evangelical megachurch . . . At one point we became the largest evangelical open and affirming church. And from there we really made a lot of shifts, and all of a sudden, I think we were something like a progressive Christian church. And then we were a rapidly declining church, and I don't know what we ended up . . . a "not church" of some sort of interfaith spiritual goulash. It's been wild, and when I think back through all of that I'm just amazed. But I also learned that the slippery slope is real.[4]*

As ECC slid down its slope, it stopped even pretending to be Christian. ECC's "interfaith spiritual goulash" embraces just about every kind of spiritual experience and belief except biblical Christianity. Meeks' website describes the church as having evolved into "a quirky interfaith (and non-faith) spiritual community with a deep appreciation for all great teachers of Love and Self-Actualization." Ryan himself raves about various forms of New Age spirituality, including reincarnation, vision quests, "conscious sexuality," and drug-induced spiritual experiences.

This is the bottom of the slippery slope: full-blown idolatry. New Age religious rituals are rooted in Hinduism, a religion absolutely saturated with idolatry. New Age rituals are always covenantal in nature, always connecting worshipers in covenant to evil spiritual forces.

In America, New Age spirituality always centers around America's central idol, the idol of self. Ryan Meeks has received a lot of revelations about himself

---

[4] EastLake Update - 9/9/20 https://www.youtube.com/watch?v=V9ocSv3fGgE&t=1473s

since he left pastoral ministry. He says, "There's a whole universe of 'Ryan' behind the persona of Pastor Ryan."

New Age worshipers eventually come to the belief that they are actually God. We are all part of the universal connected oneness that is God. All life is connected. All life is God. Ryan talks about God as being "the unitive experience of all pervasive love."

This journey that ECC has gone through encapsulates the journey many denominations have taken. Denominational schools come under the control of Jezebel. She teaches, seduces, and prophesies. Students become convinced that sexual immorality should be celebrated. They become convinced that there are many paths to God, many good religions. They start to participate in religious ceremonies that connect people to evil spiritual forces. Perhaps they take part in religious rituals associated with New Age or with Native American spirituality. They reject belief in hell and in the uniqueness of Christ's atoning sacrifice. They start to think of Jesus as just one of many great teachers. Perhaps He was actually a "woke" political activist, inspiring them to stand against the oppressors.

From these schools come the denomination's administrators, professors, scholars, schoolteachers, pastors, and political activists. As time goes on, Jezebel's disciples gain a stranglehold over the organizational hierarchy of entire denominations. When Jezebel has enough of her people in place, she drives out the true worshipers of Yahweh, refusing to allow Bible-believing Christians to have any positions of influence within the organization. Everyone must embrace her "interfaith spiritual goulash." Everyone must celebrate homosexuality and gay marriage.

The church members who fill the pews on a Sunday morning don't usually buy into all of Jezebel's new teachings. They start to leave, one by one at first, and eventually in droves. ECC experienced a severe numerical decline in church membership as they discarded biblical Christianity. Mainline denominations have experienced the same decline in a more gradual manner.

Jesus promised us that He would cast Jezebel into a sickbed and that those who commit adultery with her would enter a time of tribulation. Thankfully, denominations that embrace Jezebel will never prosper. As they slide into idolatry, they also lose influence and membership. They become diseased and weakened. Eventually they will die out, and their influence upon the body of Christ will be removed. This is God's grace to keep His church from being completely destroyed.

BIBLICAL DOCTRINE AND SEXUAL IMMORALITY

The above story speaks of churches that have come fully under the control of Jezebel. They are no longer capable of discerning between good and evil. They proclaim the goodness of idolatry and sexual immorality, acting as the very mouthpieces of Jezebel. They work to spread her system through the nation.

But what about the churches that still claim to follow biblical teaching? What about churches that still teach sexual intercourse is only intended by God for the lifelong covenant of marriage? What about churches that teach that Jesus is the way, the truth, and the life, that nobody comes to the Father except through Him (John 14:6)?

There are many, many churches that still claim to follow biblical doctrine. They have not changed the official doctrines of their churches under pressure from Jezebel. Nevertheless, many churches that have biblical doctrinal statements, that claim to believe the Bible is the inspired, inerrant word of God, are deeply compromised with Jezebel.

Jezebel teaches and seduces people into committing sexual immorality. How many Bible-believing churches are free of sexual immorality? A church can hold biblical doctrines about the sanctity of marriage and sexual sin, but what is really happening in the youth group? Studies have shown that "born-again" youth participate in premarital sexual intercourse at nearly the same rate as their non-Christian peers.[5]

And what about the adults? In 2014, the Barna Group, an evangelical Christian polling firm, polled a representative sample of three hundred eighty-eight men

[5] General Social Survey (GSS) 2014 through 2018

self-identified as Christians. Seventy-seven percent of the men aged eighteen to thirty-nine had looked at pornography at least monthly. Thirty-two percent admitted to being addicted to pornography (and another twelve percent thought they might be). A majority of married Christian men admitted to viewing pornography at least monthly. Thirty-five percent of them admitted to having had an extramarital affair. Quite simply, there is a lot of secret sexual sin taking place in nearly every church in America.

GIVING PEOPLE WHAT THEY WANT

There are many seeker-sensitive churches in America that have become more sensitive to what people want than to what God wants. Many churches have learned that if they want to grow, they must give people what they want. They teach messages of self-improvement, self-fulfillment, and self-actualization. They teach people to believe in themselves and to get what they want out of life.

There is some truth in these messages. Nevertheless, the idolatry of self is often present. And where this idolatry is present, Jezebel is also present. Churches that focus on these messages lack any real authority over the spirit of Jezebel.

Worship of the idol of self manifests in other ways. Some American churches seem to be obsessed with the attainment of financial prosperity. Some of these operate like pyramid schemes, teaching people that if they give their money to the rich guy at the top of the church organization, they will somehow become as wealthy as he is. The greed that drives these people is one of the lusts of the flesh, one of the supporting pillars of the temple in which self is worshipped.

The idol around which Jezebel is building her system is the idol of self. How many churches truly teach their people to die to themselves take up their cross, and follow Jesus? How many churches teach their people how to hear the voice of God, to put aside every other voice, so that they can faithfully follow and obey Him? How many churches train their people to lay their lives upon the altar of God so that they can receive His instructions for their life? The church that resists the control of Jezebel must actually know the voice of the Lord and obey His voice.

STRIVING FOR ACCEPTANCE

For generations, the media has portrayed Bible-believing Christians as narrow-minded, hypocritical bigots. Nobody wants to be a bigot. Christians grow up viewing these negative portrayals of Christians from Hollywood, and they have a desire to prove they are not really like that. They want to prove they've been misunderstood, that they are actually deeply caring and loving people who would do anything to help others.

In fact, Christians want to be loved and accepted by the world. They don't understand just how badly the deck is stacked against them. The enemy has created a system in which Christians will always be portrayed as the bad guys unless they compromise their biblical convictions. As long as Christians continue to believe that sin is actually sin, they will never be fully accepted in American society.

This desire for acceptance, this desire to be loved by the world, will always lead to deep compromise. The church that fears being called bigoted or narrowminded will be manipulated by the world to leave their core convictions.

This is happening at an extremely rapid rate today. Christian institutions are desperately trying to show they are not prejudiced against gays. They are desperately trying to show that they believe homosexual practice is sin but actually love gays and don't despise them. But it doesn't matter how much they love people struggling with homosexuality. Until Christians renounce their biblical convictions that homosexual practice is sin, they will be condemned by the world as bigots. It is impossible to hold on to biblical teachings about homosexuality without being called hateful, intolerant bigots.

This is the reality. There is no way to escape this accusation unless you are willing to completely change your view of Scripture and morality in general. And multitudes of Christians and Christian organizations are proving that they are willing to change their views on sexual sin in hopes of becoming more acceptable in the world's eyes.

In the end, none of these changes will make any difference. Jezebel will not be satisfied by the church that accept gays and lesbians. She will only be satisfied when the church actively celebrates homosexuality as a gift from God. She will not tolerate Bible-believing Christianity in any form. She will not allow Bible-believing Christianity to be taught in Christian schools. She will not be satisfied until every school in America teaches that homosexual lust is a good thing, a gift from God. Every school in America must teach that evil is good and good is evil.

This is the struggle that we face. The desire to be loved by the world is a great weakness in the modern church. The church must accept the fact that if she is faithful to Jesus Christ and the gospel that was given to her, she will be hated by this world.

And in fact, Jesus promised us that the world would hate us, not love us. He said, "You will be hated by everyone because of me (Matthew 10:22 NIV)." This is part of what we signed up for.

THE IDOLATRY OF RELIGIOUS TRADITION

There is a second group of churches in America that is trapped in a different kind of idolatry than the idolatry of self. Many churches in America have placed their religious traditions in the place of God. They are not focused on self-fulfillment, self-actualization, and the idols of our culture. They are focused on their traditional way of doing things and their denominations' traditional interpretations of Scripture. They are trying to hold on to their religious system.

Religious tradition can become a kind of idol that replaces the real presence and worship of God. The Pharisees in the Bible thought that they were the true worshippers of God. Jesus exposed the fact that what they really obeyed was their own set of religious traditions. Isaiah was right when he prophesied about you hypocrites; as it is written:

"These people honor me with their lips, but their hearts are far from me. They worship me in vain; their teachings are merely human rules." *You have let go of the commands of God and are holding on to human traditions. (Mark 7:6-8 NIV)*

There are many churches in a similar condition today. Everything they do is determined by the traditions and rules of their usually conservative denomination. If Baptist, they worship God in the Baptist way, read the favored Baptist scriptures, explain the Scripture in the traditional Baptist way, sing Baptist songs, and have church government structured in the Baptist way. The same could be said for Anabaptists or Brethren or Reformed or other traditional denominations.

But where is the Holy Spirit in all of this? Is it possible to follow a denominational system, doing everything according to the pattern of your denomination, without actually knowing God, without ever hearing and obeying His voice? Is it possible to attend a church that supposedly believes all the right stuff, but the presence of God is just not there?

I believe it is possible. I grew up attending church every Sunday. I sort of believed all the right things. Yet I never once felt the Lord's presence during my childhood years. I don't think I knew the Lord at all until He met me in my late teens. I think there might be many "Christians" who are in the same condition.

The point is this. Jezebel has deeply corrupted the American church. She has erected the idol of self in many churches, and the idolatry of religious traditions in others. She has brought sexual immorality in one form or another into nearly every church.

THE TEST

Jesus prophesied about the time of trouble that would come upon churches that have compromised with Jezebel. He said of Jezebel:

> *Indeed I will cast her into a sickbed, and those who commit adultery with her into great tribulation, unless they repent of their deeds. (Revelation 2:22 NKJV)*

This time of tribulation, this time of great testing, is upon us. Jesus also prophesied about this test in His well-known Sermon on the Mount.

> *Therefore whoever hears these sayings of Mine, and does them, I will liken him to a wise man who built his house on the rock: and the rain descended, the floods came, and the winds blew and beat on that house; and it did not fall, for it was founded on the rock. But everyone who hears these sayings of Mine, and does not do them, will be like a foolish man who built his house on the sand: and the rain descended, the floods came, and the winds blew and beat on that house; and it fell. And great was its fall. (Matthew 7:24-27 NKJV)*

We can compare churches and denominations today to houses that human beings have built. If the builders heard the word of God and obeyed His voice, these houses will stand when the test comes, the time of tribulation and trouble Jesus described in Revelation 2:22. If the builders did not hear and obey, the houses will suddenly collapse.

I believe that in the days ahead God will allow a time of testing to come upon His church. Jezebel will unleash a season of persecution upon those who believe in the word of God. Many churches and denominations that seem strong will collapse in this test.

THE SWORD OF THE SPIRIT

What is the word of God? How do we build houses that will stand the test? The apostle Paul's description of the armor of God (Ephesians 6:10-18) speaks of the Christian's ultimate weapon, i.e., "the sword of the Spirit, which is the word of God" (Ephesians 6:17).

The word of God is more than just the written Word, the Bible. The word of God is the written Word wielded by the Spirit of God. We need both the written Word and the Spirit of God if we hope to obey God's word.

If we don't have the Spirit of God, we don't actually have the word of God because the word of God is the sword of the Spirit. Even the devil quoted scripture, but he did not do so by the Spirit of God. Therefore, he didn't actually have the word of God. The Pharisees had the written Word but not the Spirit of God. Therefore, they did not actually have the word of God, and their house was not built upon the rock. When the test came, the entire religious system of the Pharisees collapsed. The Roman armies destroyed the religious system of the Pharisees in AD 70.

There are many churches today that are missing the Spirit of God despite the biblical doctrines to which they ascribe. How is this possible?

BLASPHEMING THE HOLY SPIRIT

Jesus spoke of one sin that is greater than any other, a sin that cannot be forgiven in this life or in the life to come. This great sin is speaking against the Holy Spirit, the blasphemy of the Holy Spirit.

Blasphemy of the Holy Spirit can take two forms. The first form we have already discussed. When people claim that the Spirit of God is leading them to do something evil, they are committing a kind of blasphemy. If someone says that the Spirit of God is telling him to leave his wife and marry another woman, he is blaspheming, using the Lord's name in vain. If church leaders declare that the Spirit of God is leading them to embrace homosexuality and gay marriage, they are blaspheming. This is the sin that ECC committed when it claimed that Christ was the one leading them to embrace homosexual behavior.

There is another form of blasphemy discussed in the New Testament. In the account of Matthew 12:22-32, Jesus performed a great miracle, healing a man who was demon-possessed, blind, and mute. When the Pharisees witnessed this great miracle, they claimed that Jesus was casting out demons with the power of Beelzebub, the ruler of the demons. Jesus responded to their claims:

> *If Satan casts out Satan, he is divided against himself. How then will his kingdom stand?... But if I cast out demons by the Spirit of God, surely the kingdom of God has come upon you ... Therefore I say to you, every sin and blasphemy will be forgiven men, but the blasphemy against the Spirit will not be forgiven men. Anyone who speaks a word against the Son of Man, it will be forgiven him; but whoever speaks against the Holy Spirit, it will not be forgiven him, either in this age or in the age to come. (Matthew 12:26, 28, 31-32 NKJV)*

In this passage, God gave the people a precious gift, a powerful miracle performed right in front of them. The Pharisees insisted that Jesus did this miracle with the power of Beelzebub. Jesus stated that He did this miracle by the Spirit of God. Then He gave the Pharisees perhaps the most severe warning in history, telling them that if they spoke against the Spirit of God in the way they were doing, they would not be forgiven in this age or in the age to come.

In other words, when God does a precious work by the power of the Holy Spirit in front of someone, there is actually a great danger. If the witness of this work declares that this work of God is actually the work of the devil, he is speaking against the Holy Spirit. He cannot be forgiven.

What happens when God's Spirit visits a church and does miracles among the people? What if the Spirit moves as it did in the day of Pentecost and people appear drunk because they are speaking in other languages? What happens when people don't actually accept the work of the Spirit of God?

When the Holy Spirit moves in a special way, it brings a kind of test to the people. Those who love the Spirit of God value the work of the Spirit. They receive it and treasure it. But some are tempted to speak against the work of the Holy Spirit. Perhaps they prefer to follow a system of rules and traditions. Perhaps they don't like it when God shows up.

If people commit the sin of blasphemy against the Holy Spirit by speaking against the Holy Spirit and calling it demonic, they cannot be forgiven. I think that when people are in danger of committing this blasphemy, the Holy Spirit often leaves their presence before they fully cross over the line and blaspheme against the Holy Spirit.

In this way, the Holy Spirit leaves churches and denominations when their members begin to criticize the work of the Spirit. God doesn't want them to commit the sin that cannot be forgiven. So in His mercy, the Holy Spirit simply leaves before the people commit this sin. A kind of judgment settles upon those churches. They talk about God, but the Holy Spirit is no longer there. The church becomes dry and lifeless. If you visit that church, you will not find Spirit of God present.

There may be many churches in this category. They follow their set of rules and traditions. They claim to believe in biblical doctrines, but the Holy Spirit is not actually there because of the way the people treated Him. They murmured against Him and His work. They didn't value or seek His gifts or His presence. And so He removes His presence from them before they end up committing blasphemy.

The Bible speaks of the "quenching" of the Holy Spirit: "Do not quench the Spirit" (I Thessalonians 5:19). It is possible for the fire of the Holy Spirit to be quenched, causing the Holy Spirit to leave. What happens to such a church when a time of persecution comes? If they do not have the Spirit of God in their midst, they do not actually have the word of God, which is the sword of the Spirit. If they don't have the word of God, they cannot build upon the rock. The rains fall, the floods rise, the winds blow and beat against the house, and it suddenly collapses.

When the time of testing comes to the church in America, it will become very evident if we have built upon the rock or not. It will become evident if the churches are actually obeying the word of God, if they actually believe and obey both the written Word and the Spirit of God. Churches that have been built by the religious mind of man for the glory of man will suddenly collapse.

It may appear for a time that Jezebel is victorious in America as many churches fail to stand during the storm that is approaching. We may see a falling away, a collapse of many Christian institutions. But thank God that just as during the worst days of Jezebel's persecution there were still those faithful to Yahweh (1 Kings 19:18), God has many true disciples in the United States.

Some will pass the test. In fact, the coming season of testing will be a time of great strengthening for the true church. A church will arise that is firmly built upon the rock, a church that holds on to the written Word of God. It will be a church that clearly hears the voice of God and obeys that voice wholeheartedly. In the last days, everything that can be shaken will be shaken (Hebrews 12:27), but this church will be unshakeable.

Chapter Fifteen

THE LORD'S ARMY

As I have explained the work of Jezebel in our nation's government, churches, schools, and families, it might seem that her plans are unassailable. In fact, Jezebel will be defeated. Although Jezebel's army is vast and well trained, it will ultimately lose the battle for America's future.

The Lord God has an army that is greater than Jezebel's army because God Himself is with His army. When Jezebel's servants ruled the land of Israel, the situation looked so grim that even the prophet Elijah entered a time of depression, as we described in chapter six. In his depressed condition, Elijah said to God:

> *I have been very zealous for the LORD God of hosts; for the children of Israel have forsaken Your covenant, torn down Your altars, and killed Your prophets with the sword. I alone am left; and they seek to take my life. (1 Kings 19:10 NKJV).*

God responded by instructing Elijah to anoint his successors, Elisha, Hazael, and Jehu, the mighty men who would finish the work Elijah was becoming too discouraged to do. He also told Elijah that in fact there were thousands of Israelites who had refused to worship Baal.

> *Yet I have reserved seven thousand in Israel, all whose knees have not bowed to Baal, and every mouth that has not kissed him. (1 Kings 19:18 NKJV)*

God's army was already present in Israel. Although most Israelites failed the test and compromised with Jezebel's system of Baal worship, seven thousand had passed the test by refusing to form idolatrous covenants with Baal. In refusing to participate in these covenants, they risked their lives and proved that their covenant with Yahweh meant everything to them.

Likewise in America, though much of the church is deeply corrupted by sexual immorality and the worship of self, God has servants who are completely dedicated to Him. These true worshipers are His army. They will not compromise with Jezebel. They will risk everything they have in the battle with Jezebel. And in the end, Jezebel and her religious system will be driven from our land.

God gives us a wonderful promise in the apostle Paul's second epistle to the church of Corinth.

> For the weapons of our warfare are not carnal but mighty in God for pulling down strongholds, casting down arguments and every high thing that exalts itself against the knowledge of God, bringing every thought into captivity to the obedience of Christ, and being ready to punish all disobedience when your obedience is fulfilled. (2 Corinthians 10:4-6 NKJV)

God will punish all disobedience once His people have fulfilled their obedience. When His servants are completely obedient, He releases judgment upon the strongholds of the evil one.

THE WAR IN HEAVEN

In Revelation 12, we read about a war taking place in the spiritual realms between the devil and his angels and the archangel Michael and his angels. We read about the victory in this war as Michael's heavenly army casts down the devil and his angels from their positions of authority in the heavenly realms.

> And war broke out in heaven: Michael and his angels fought with the dragon; and the dragon and his angels fought, but they did not prevail,

nor was a place found for them in heaven any longer. So the great dragon was cast out, that serpent of old, called the Devil and Satan, who deceives the whole world; he was cast to the earth, and his angels were cast out with him. Then I heard a loud voice saying in heaven, "Now salvation, and strength, and the kingdom of our God, and the power of His Christ have come, for the accuser of our brethren, who accused them before our God day and night, has been cast down. And they overcame him by the blood of the Lamb and by the word of their testimony, and they did not love their lives to the death." (Revelation 12:7-11 NKJV)

The devil and his angels are the evil spiritual rulers who empower every evil spiritual and religious system. These are the rulers of the darkness of this age who work to keep the earth in spiritual darkness. When they fall, the religious and governmental systems the devil uses to rule this earth lose their authority. They lose their ability to keep the earth trapped in lies and spiritual darkness.

When these rulers are cast down, the heavens open and the revelation of God fills the earth, resulting in great harvest. I teach about this opening of the heavens and the resulting spiritual harvest in my book *Open Heavens: A Biblical Guide to High-Level Spiritual Warfare.*

This scripture passage doesn't just speak about Michael's army of angels. It also speaks about an army of overcomers on the earth who "overcame by the blood of the lamb, by the word of their testimony, and they loved not their lives to the death" (v. 11).

This earthly army is not an army of angels but of people. The actions of this army are the driving force behind the victory that takes place in the heavenly realms. We know this because the army overcomes by "the blood of the Lamb." Jesus died for people, not for angels. It is human beings, not angels, who are able to enter into a covenant with God through the blood of Jesus Christ that was shed at the cross. It is human beings who overcome by the blood of the Lamb.

This is the army that will defeat Jezebel and all the forces of darkness. It is an army that overcomes in the three-fold way that is described in Revelation 12:11. They overcame:

- By the blood of the Lamb.
- By the word of their testimony.
- They loved not their lives to the death (KJV).

This scripture verse is speaking about those who walk in covenant with the Most High God and are willing to pay the price of that covenant. They are willing to testify, to speak the word of God, even if costs them their life. They love the Lord their God more than their life.

THEY OVERCAME BY THE BLOOD OF THE LAMB

Jezebel works primarily by convincing people to form blood covenants with her idols through blood sacrifices and sexual immorality. Jezebel is defeated primarily through blood covenant as well. Our Lord's army has a blood covenant with Him formed by the blood of Jesus Christ as Jesus Himself declared when He shared the cup at the Last Supper.

> For this is My blood of the new covenant, which is shed for many for the remission of sins. (Matthew 26:28 NKJV; see also Luke 22:20)

> In the same manner He also took the cup after supper, saying, "This cup is the new covenant in My blood. This do, as often as you drink it, in remembrance of Me." (1 Corinthians 11:25 NKJV)

This new covenant in the blood of Christ is infinitely stronger than any evil covenant. In the new covenant, men and women are connected to the living God. They become one with the living God. All the resources of heaven are made available to them.

Much of the American church is too compromised to be a part of this army. It is impossible to walk in the full authority of our covenant with Jesus Christ when we have formed covenants with the evil one. There are many preachers who preach the right things but live in a way that they are stripped of real spiritual authority.

The church that has formed covenants with the devil is completely unable to rule with Christ over the earth. The church that has formed covenants with darkness will always be manipulated and oppressed by the evil one. They become a part of Jezebel's network of influence and control, puppets and pawns who are manipulated by their covenant partners, unable to bring about real change on the earth. These compromised Christians are not actually part of God's army. They have no capability of taking effective action against Jezebel because they are not willing to pay the cost of their covenant with God.

The members of God's army give themselves completely to His covenant. They are free of the unholy covenantal connections that are formed through sexual immorality and idolatry. They believe in the Lord and live for the Lord.

In practical terms, what does this mean? If you desire to be part of God's army, your life must be free from evil covenants. It is necessary to do a spiritual housecleaning, repenting of any connections to darkness. This may include repentance of past experimentation with the occult, astrology, or New Age practices. It may include repentance from participation in religious rituals with false religions, masturbation, pornography, and immoral relationships from the past.

All of these sins are covenantal. When you join the army of the Lord God of Hosts, you belong to Him. Every unholy connection must be repented of and broken. Evil spirits that have control or influence over your life must be driven out.

Every overcomer must be fully committed to their covenant with God. They need to understand the foundational Christian doctrines that are part of this covenant as described in Hebrews 6:1-3, which include "repenting from evil deeds and placing our faith in God . . . baptisms, the laying on of hands, the resurrection of the dead, and eternal judgment" (NLT).

BY THE WORD OF THEIR TESTIMONY

Secondly, God's army must know God's Word and speak the word of God. The overcomers overcome the evil one by the word of their testimony. As we discussed in the previous chapter, "the sword of the Spirit, which is the word of God" (Ephesians 6:17) is not just the written Word. We need the written Word and the Spirit of God. Only then can we overcome the evil one by the word of our testimony.

God's army must know the written Word. When we are involved in spiritual warfare, the devil often quotes Scripture and twists Scripture. He quoted Scripture to Jesus Himself during the temptation in the wilderness (Matthew 4:1-11), taking Jesus to a pinnacle of the temple and saying:

> *If You are the Son of God, throw Yourself down. For it is written: "He shall give His angels charge over you," and, "In their hands they shall bear you up, lest you dash your foot against a stone." (Matthew 4:6-7)*

Jesus responded with the words:

> *It is written again, "You shall not tempt the Lord your God." (Matthew 4:7)*

As Jesus quoted the written Word, He did so by the Spirit of God. Therefore, His words carried the authority of God to break the deception of the evil one. It is God's Word spoken with the power of the Spirit of God that destroys deception. Those who are members of God's overcoming army must know the voice of the Spirit of God and the power of the Spirit of God. Before His ascension, Jesus promised His disciples that when the Holy Spirit came upon them, they would receive power to be witnesses, power to testify.

> *But you shall receive power when the Holy Spirit has come upon you; and you shall be witnesses to Me in Jerusalem, and in all Judea and Samaria, and to the end of the earth. (Acts 1:8 NKJV)*

Without the Holy Spirit, there is no effective testimony. Without the Holy Spirit, we will not win victories. Our testimony is our sword, our primary offensive weapon in our battle against Jezebel and her army. We must learn to speak the word of God clearly and powerfully under the inspiration of the Holy Spirit.

The word of God must be confirmed by the power of God. When Jesus sent out His disciples to testify, He didn't send them empty handed. He sent them with divine power telling them:

> *Heal the sick, raise the dead, cleanse those who have leprosy, drive out demons. Freely you have received; freely give. (Matthew 10:8 NKJV)*

His disciples received the power of God. Consequently, they gave the people miracles from that same power. In practical terms, if you want to become effective in the battle against Jezebel, you must know the word of God. You need to study the written Word and seek to know the power and voice of the Holy Spirit. Only then can you properly use the sword of the Spirit, the word of God. Only then can you have an impact in the battle against Jezebel.

THEY LOVED NOT THEIR LIVES TO THE DEATH

Perhaps even more important than speaking God's word with power is speaking God's word with love. The overcomers in the book of Revelation "loved not their lives unto death" (KJV). In other words, they loved God and the people to whom they testified more than their own lives.

This is the love that is at the very center of Christianity. The love demonstrated at the cross of Jesus Christ. God's army must learn to walk in the same sacrificial love that Christ walked in or it will not defeat Jezebel.

When Jesus prophesied to His disciples that He was about to go to the cross, where this great love would be demonstrated, Peter pulled Jesus aside to rebuke Him. Jesus turned and spoke strongly to Peter.

> *"Get behind Me, Satan! You are an offense to Me, for you are not mindful of the things of God, but the things of men." Then Jesus said to His disciples, "If anyone desires to come after Me, let him deny himself, and take up his cross, and follow Me. For whoever desires to save his life will lose it, but whoever loses his life for My sake will find it." (Matthew 16:23-25 NKJV)*

There are two sides to our covenant with God just as there are two sides to every covenant. On the one side, our Lord Jesus Christ gave His life for us on the cross. The cross was the covenant altar where the cost of covenant was paid. On the other side, Jesus tells us that there is also a cross for us. He said to His disciples, "Anyone who comes after me must deny himself, take up his cross, and follow after me."

The church that only emphasizes the blessings of our covenant with God but not the price of our covenant will never walk in the full authority of that covenant. The church that only emphasizes the blessings of the covenant can be compared to a man who only wants to experience the fun part of marriage with his wife but not pay the price of marriage. He enjoys the honeymoon and the bedroom but doesn't want to work and serve his family. Such a marriage will never become what God wants it to be. It will never become the center of a strong family.

In the same way, so many churches in America only want to emphasize the blessings of our covenant with God but not the cost of the covenant. They talk endlessly about all that God gives us—salvation, forgiveness, spiritual gifts, peace, and prosperity. They do not talk about the cost of covenant. They do not talk about the cross that true believers need to carry. If you follow Jesus, there is much blessing, peace, joy, and even prosperity. And yet if you obey Him completely and completely walk out His plan for your life, it will cost you everything.

WHAT IS THE CROSS?

What is the cross that Jesus asks us to carry? First of all, the cross represents the supernatural love of God. The cross is ultimately the greatest demonstration of God's love. At the cross, God showed just how much He loved us. True love, God's love, is revealed at the cross.

Second, the cross is obedience to the point of death because of love. The cross is the place where we die to our own will and choose God's will. The cross is the altar where the price of covenant is paid. When you take up your cross, you pray as Jesus did: "Lord, not my will, but Your will be done" (Matthew 26:39; Mark 14:36; Luke 22:42). You kill your own plans, ambitions, and desires and give yourself completely to God's will no matter the cost, no matter where He sends you, no matter what He asks you to do.

Third, the cross is extreme humility because of love. Jesus hung naked on the cross, suffering the most humiliating death imaginable because of love. Those who take up their cross no longer live for themselves and their own reputation and honor. They are willing to humble themselves and serve without reward in the most difficult places on this earth.

THE DENIAL OF SELF

Jesus said, "If anyone desires to come after Me, let him deny himself, and take up his cross, and follow Me." Jezebel's principal idol in America is the idol of self. The cross represents the denial of self. The cross is casting down the idol of self so that one can do the will of God. It involves paying a price because of your love for someone other than yourself.

In practical terms, what can you do to be part of God's army? Seek to know the love of God and be willing to pay a price because of that love. Be willing to pay a price to help those whom God brings into your life as you seek to love your neighbor as yourself. Set aside your own desires and live for the One who gave everything for you.

Put every major decision upon the altar of God as you seek to obey His voice and align yourself with His purposes. Don't be led by ambition, money, or even family expectations. Seek God until He answers and speaks to your heart. Spend hours and days in prayer, worshiping and waiting upon the Lord until He speaks. When He speaks to your heart, obey His instructions wholeheartedly.

We must learn to testify, to speak the word of the Lord, to a nation that is enveloped in darkness. Faith comes from hearing and hearing from the word of God (Romans 10:17). If the gospel is not preached, the darkness remains. If we hope to see people delivered from the systems and lies of Jezebel, we must become very bold in speaking the truth, calling them to repentance and faith in Jesus Christ. The overcomers overcome by "the word of their testimony."

This is the path of obedience and love. If you walk it, God will use you powerfully in the coming battle.

TRAINING THE LORD GOD OF HOST'S ARMY

Churches that are effective in this war in the days ahead might look more like schools than churches. They will train their people to be disciples of Christ. They will train their people to know God and His voice. They will teach their people to spend hours in prayer seeking the Lord, waiting upon Him until He speaks and gives each person his or her assignment. They will train their people to know the foundational doctrines of the faith.

The leaders of these training centers must demonstrate what they are teaching. A good tree produces good fruit. Leaders must produce fruit of their own before they are allowed to train others. They need to be men and women of action who lead by example as they hear and obey God's voice. They will pay a higher price and take more risks than those they are training just as the apostles did in the early church.

So many churches offer a kind of entertainment to their members. They offer professional performances with uplifting messages and good music. The sanctuary chairs are so relaxing. There are coffee shops, sports facilities, and social events for the youth. Attending church is so easy, comfortable, and entertaining.

That is all going to change. The leading churches in our nation will no longer be those that are the most comfortable and entertaining. The leading churches will be those whose leaders pay the highest price and teach their people to pay the price. The leading ministries will be those who are fearless and bold, willing to confront the works of Jezebel as they take up their cross and follow Jesus.

Chapter Sixteen

REVEALING A HOLY GOD

Our Lord Jesus Christ reveals Himself in different ways at different times to different people according to the revelation they need. He is the Savior to those who need to be saved, to those who call on His name. He is the Shepherd for the sheep and the Lamb of God for those who need His perfect sacrifice. He is the Healer for those who need healing. He is all these things and much more.

In the book of Revelation, Jesus Christ reveals Himself in a different way to each of the seven churches described in chapters 2 and 3 according to what they needed to overcome the tests they faced. So how does He reveal himself to the church of Thyatira, which had allowed Jezebel to teach, seduce and prophesy?

> *To the angel of the church in Thyatira write: "These are the words of the Son of God, whose eyes are like blazing fire and whose feet are like burnished bronze." (Revelation 2:18, NIV)*

Our Lord's eyes are like flames of fire and His feet like brightly polished metal. His feet are further described in Revelation 1:15 as appearing "like bronze glowing in a furnace." In other words, Christ comes to the church of Thyatira with the fire of His holy presence. If we understand this revelation of Christ, we will be equipped to defeat Jezebel and her idols.

EXPOSING, PURIFYING, AND DESTROYING

God's holy fire works in three primary ways. It exposes, purifies, and destroys. When you see fire at a distance, you don't feel its heat, but you see its light. During biblical times, there was no electricity, so any lights that burned at night were actually fires.

The blazing fire in the eyes of Jesus represents the exposing work of this fire. Nothing can hide from God's sight. His gaze penetrates into every hidden thing, every hidden sin, even the hidden motives of men's hearts. His eyes penetrate every deception of Jezebel. He exposes the filthiness of her works and deeds, her abominations and fornication. She pretends to be a prophetess, but she is in fact both a witch and a whore.

Secondly, we have the refining work of fire. The Son of God revealed Himself to the church of Thyatira with feet of bronze glowing in the furnace. Metal is refined in fire. Metal that has passed through the fire has been cleansed of its impurities. Everything that is not metal is burned up in the fire, leaving behind the pure metal. In the same way, the fire of God burns away the impurities that are in human hearts until those hearts belong completely to Him.

Thirdly, we have the judgments of God that destroy the works of darkness. In this passage, we read about the feet of Christ as purified bronze still glowing from the furnace. Bronze is a hardened metal, representing God's intolerance and judgment of sin. Sin must be punished, must be paid for. In the tabernacle of Moses, the bronze altar was the place where sacrifices were offered for the atonement of sin so that the judgments of God would not break forth against the people.

Likewise, God's feet are often referred to in the Bible as instruments of His judgments. Throughout Scripture, there are references to the wicked being trampled under His feet, often with the imagery of trampling grapes in a winepress.

> *I [God] have trodden the winepress alone, and from the peoples no one was with Me. For I have trodden them in My anger, and trampled them in My fury; their blood is sprinkled upon My garments, and I have*

stained all My robes. For the day of vengeance is in My heart, and the year of My redeemed has come (Isaiah 63:3-4 NKJV).

You [God] will tread down the wicked, for they will be ashes under the soles of Your feet on that day. (Malachi 4:3 NASB)

The God of peace will soon crush Satan under your feet. (Romans 16:20 NIV)

In Revelation 14:19-20, the "vine of the earth" is thrown into the great winepress of the wrath of God. The grapes are trampled, and blood flows from the winepress like a river for a distance of fourteen hundred furlongs (two hundred miles). When we read about the Lord Jesus coming with feet of bronze, it is a picture of His judgments. He is coming to judge the wicked, to trample them under His feet.

The church of Thyatira needed this revelation. God is coming to judge the earth. She needed to know God's hatred and intolerance of sin. The works of Jezebel will not be allowed to continue. They will be exposed. Some will be purified by the fire of God. Those who refuse to repent will be destroyed by the same fire.

ELIJAH AND THE FIRE OF GOD

Elijah the prophet was sent by God to confront Jezebel and her religious and political system. Elijah brought the fire of God to Israel. This fire exposed the idolatry of Israel as Elijah demonstrated the difference between Yahweh and Baal. The fire worked to refine and purify the people, bringing them to repentance and faith in God. The fire also brought destruction to all who hardened their heats.

We read about Elijah's ministry of judgment and fire in the confrontation on Mount Carmel described in chapters seventeen and eighteen of 1 Kings. In this account, Elijah confronted King Ahab because of his idolatry, telling the king:

> *As the LORD God of Israel lives, before whom I stand, there shall not be dew nor rain these years, except at my word. (1 Kings 17:1 NKJV)*

For three years it did not rain, and severe famine came to Israel. After the third year, God told Elijah to present himself to Ahab, and Ahab drove out to confront Elijah (1 Kings 18).

The king said to Elijah, "Is that you, O troubler of Israel?" (v. 17). Elijah responded:

> *I have not troubled Israel, but you and your father's house have, in that you have forsaken the commandments of the LORD and have followed the Baals. Now therefore, send and gather all Israel to me on Mount Carmel, the four hundred and fifty prophets of Baal, and the four hundred prophets of Asherah, who eat at Jezebel's table. (vv. 18-19)*

So, the children of Israel and the prophets of Baal met together on Mount Carmel. There Elijah confronted the people.

> *How long will you falter between two opinions? If the LORD is God, follow Him; but if Baal, follow him. (v. 21)*

Nobody answered him. Then Elijah spoke again.

> *I alone am left a prophet of the LORD; but Baal's prophets are four hundred and fifty men. Therefore, let them give us two bulls; and let them choose one bull for themselves, cut it in pieces, and lay it on the wood, but put no fire under it; and I will prepare the other bull, and lay it on the wood, but put no fire under it. Then you call on the name of your gods, and I will call on the name of the LORD; and the God who answers by fire, He is God. (vv. 22-24)*

The prophets of Baal took their bull, lay it on the altar, and called upon Baal from morning until noon with the cries, "O Baal, hear us." Meanwhile, Elijah mocked them.

Cry aloud, for he is a god; either he is meditating, or he is busy, or he is on a journey, or perhaps he is sleeping and must be awakened. (v. 27)

To show their dedication to Baal and their blood covenants with him, the prophets of Baal began cutting themselves as they danced around and prophesied. Finally evening came. Elijah called the people to himself. He built the altar of the Lord with twelve stones representing the twelve tribes of Israel. He prepared the wood and sacrifice, cutting the bull into pieces. He built a trench around the altar.

Then he ordered four large waterpots to be filled with water, and had them dumped on the sacrifice and the wood. Three times the pots were poured out on the sacrifice until the water overflowed and filled the trench. Then Elijah prayed.

LORD God of Abraham, Isaac, and Israel, let it be known this day that You are God in Israel and I am Your servant, and that I have done all these things at Your word. Hear me, O LORD, hear me, that this people may know that You are the LORD God, and that You have turned their hearts back to You again. (vv. 36-37)

The fire of God fell, consuming the burnt sacrifice, wood, stones, and even the water. When the people saw it, they fell on their faces, crying out, "The Lord, He is God! The Lord, He is God!"

Elijah immediately ordered them, "Seize the prophets of Baal! Do not let them escape!"

The people seized the prophets of Baal, brought them down to the Brook Kidron, and executed them.

In this story, we see the exposing effects of Elijah's ministry. Elijah confronted Israel's idolatry. He exposed the difference between Yahweh and Baal. The people witnessed the powerlessness of Baal's prophets and their rituals when confronted with the power of Yahweh. They witnessed the fire of God that fell from heaven. Everyone learned that Yahweh was not the same as Baal.

We also see the purifying and refining fire that burned in Elijah's ministry. Elijah worked with the judgments of God to bring the people back to God. He did not allow Israel to worship idols without consequence. He humbled the nation by stopping the rain from falling. Then after three years of this hardship, he confronted the prophets of Baal on Mount Carmel, and fire fell from heaven. When this happened, the people turned their hearts back to God, crying out, "The Lord, He is God!"

We can also see the destroying fire burning in Elijah's ministry. The evil prophets of Baal were put to death. This can be compared to God trampling his enemies with feet of bronze.

JOHN THE BAPTIST AND THE FIRE OF GOD

In the New Testament, we read of another "Elijah" who worked to bring the Jewish people back to God. John the Baptist came in "the spirit and power of Elijah" (Luke 1:17) to prepare the people for the coming of the Messiah.

In the story of John, we see several parallels to the story of Elijah. Like Elijah, John struggled with depression, at one point sending men to question Jesus as to whether He was really the Christ (Luke 7:18-23). Like Elijah, John struggled with Jezebel. He confronted the sexual immorality of King Herod, who had married his brother's wife Herodias. In response, Herodias manipulated Herod into ordering John's execution just as Jezebel manipulated King Ahab (Matthew 14:1-12).

And like Elijah, John brought the fire of God to the land of Israel. First of all, he brought the exposing fire, the light of God into the land. Jesus Himself said of John:

> *He was a burning and shining lamp, and you were willing for a time to rejoice in his light. (John 5:35, NLT)*

John also exposed and confronted the sin of Israel, calling them to repentance.

> *In those days John the Baptist came preaching in the wilderness of Judea, and saying, "Repent, for the kingdom of heaven is at hand!" (Matthew 3:1-2 NIV)*

People from Jerusalem, Judea, and the region around the Jordan went out into the desert where John was preaching (Matthew 3:5-6). Many repented, confessed their sins, and were baptized by John in the Jordan River. Religious people, including the Pharisees and Sadducees, also came to see what John was doing. But they did not repent. John confronted them severely, warning them that judgment was coming.

> *Brood of vipers! Who warned you to flee from the wrath to come? Therefore bear fruits worthy of repentance . . . And even now the ax is laid to the root of the trees. Therefore every tree which does not bear good fruit is cut down and thrown into the fire. (Matthew 3:7b-10 NKJV)*

John also prophesied about the One coming after him Who would completely immerse His listeners in the holy fire of God.

I indeed baptize you with water unto repentance, but He who is coming after me is mightier than I, whose sandals I am not worthy to carry. He will baptize you with the Holy Spirit and fire. His winnowing fan is in His hand, and He will thoroughly clean out His threshing floor, and gather His wheat into the barn; but He will burn up the chaff with unquenchable fire." (Matthew 3:11-12 NKJV)

John's message could be summed up in the words: "The fire is coming! It will either destroy you or it will baptize you!" And the fire indeed came as John prophesied. On the day of Pentecost, described in Acts 2, believers in Jesus Christ were baptized in the Holy Spirit and fire.

THE PURIFYING FIRE OF PENTECOST

There are many "Pentecostal" churches today that claim to experience the same baptism in the Holy Spirit and fire we read about in Acts 2. These churches are the spiritual descendants of the Pentecostal movement that began at Azusa Street, Los Angeles, in 1906 when a group of one hundred twenty believers were praying and waiting upon the Lord, believing that the Holy Spirit would be poured out as it was on the day of Pentecost in Acts 2. Sure enough, the Holy Spirit was poured out, and people began to speak in other tongues. The Pentecostal movement was born, and it quickly spread throughout the earth.

The Pentecostal movement emphasizes the gifts of the Holy Spirit, including gifts of tongues, healing, knowledge, and prophecy. Untold millions have come to salvation through this movement. Nevertheless, this modern Pentecostal movement seems quite different from the events that took place on the Day of Pentecost as described in Acts 2. Let's take a look at those events now.

After the resurrection of Jesus, one hundred twenty believers gathered in an upper room to wait for the outpouring of the Holy Spirit that Jesus promised.

> *And suddenly there came a sound from heaven, as of a rushing mighty wind, and it filled the whole house where they were sitting. Then there appeared to them divided tongues, as of fire, and one sat upon each of them. And they were all filled with the Holy Spirit and began to speak with other tongues, as the Spirit gave them utterance. (Acts 2:2-4 NKJV)*

Similar to the events at Azusa Street, those present at the biblical Pentecost spoke in other tongues. However, John had prophesied that Jesus would baptize people in the "Holy Spirit and fire" (Matthew 3:11). At the biblical Pentecost, fire came upon each person's head, at which point they were all filled with the Holy Spirit and began to speak in tongues. The biblical Pentecost was a baptism in the Holy Spirit and fire, that involved more than just receiving the gifts of the Holy Spirit. The believers were transformed by that fire, and the gospel spread quickly through Jerusalem, then into the nations.

In other words, the biblical Pentecost was more than just speaking in tongues. The modern Pentecostal movement emphasizes tongues and other spiritual gifts, but it seems to be missing the fire that burned at Pentecost. When

God's fire burned at Pentecost, some very unusual things began to happen. The apostle Peter preached a scorching message that exposed the sin of the nation and glorified Jesus Christ. Listeners were cut to the heart, and they began to cry out, "What shall we do?"

Peter responded:

> *Repent, and let every one of you be baptized in the name of Jesus Christ for the remission of sins; and you shall receive the gift of the Holy Spirit. (Acts 4:38 NKJV)*

Those who gladly received Peter's words were baptized, about three thousand in number. They too were filled with the Holy Spirit. These believers met daily, breaking bread together, praying together, and listening to God's Word preached by the apostles. The presence of God was so overwhelming in these times of fellowship together that the listeners' hearts burned with a desire to do God's will and give everything for Him (Acts 4:40-47).

Among the believers baptized in fire were some farmers. A family farm is a valuable possession, representing one's inheritance, livelihood, and future. Like Naboth's vineyard, that farm might have might have been given to a man's ancestors at the time of Joshua's conquest more than twelve hundred years earlier and passed down from generation to generation.

Yet when the fire of God burned in the hearts of these farmers, this great possession suddenly seemed to have little value compared to the kingdom of heaven. Farmers went home, sold their farms, and gave away the proceeds. The only thing that mattered was to do the will of God, to give everything for Him. Others did the same with houses and other valuable possessions (Acts 5:32-37).

This is the fire of God. It destroyed the love of money that lived in people's hearts. Even the greatest possessions seemed to have no value compared to God's kingdom.

That same fire destroyed the fear of man. Fearful, cowardly men and women became bold as lions as the fire burned away their fear. We see the effects of this fire in the life of the apostle Peter. After Jesus was arrested, Peter was intimidated by the words of a young girl who accused him of being a follower of Jesus (Luke 22:54-62). He denied Christ because of this fear of man. But once the fire of Pentecost burned in his heart, Peter became fearless, confronting his nation that very same day with one of the most powerful sermons ever preached (Acts 2).

This is the cleansing, purifying, refining fire of God. This is the baptism of fire in which one is immersed in that fire. The fire burns away every idol of the heart as love for God fills one's whole being. One's heart becomes consumed with the desire to worship God with all that one has, to give everything for God and to do God's will.

There is a level of God's presence so intense, so overwhelming, that it is frightening. If you stay in that presence, you need to completely obey God and give all that you have to Him. This is the presence that is in the throne room of heaven where twenty-four elders cast their crowns before the throne of God, crying:

> You are worthy, O Lord, to receive glory and honor and power; for You created all things, and by Your will they exist and were created. (Revelation 4:11 NKJV)

These crowns represent all the position and honor the elders have been given. When they see the glory of the Lord, their consuming desire is to give it all back to God in worshipful surrender.

This wholehearted, consuming worship is as frightening to a normal person as it is wonderful. It is frightening to think of completely obeying God, to give all of one's being to Him. It is frightening to think of living totally for Him, of giving up everything for Him, of going wherever He sends you to do whatever He asks you to do.

At a distance, we see the light of a fire. As we come closer to a fire, we feel its warmth. People love to sit around a fire at a respectful distance. Yet to actually enter the fire, to be immersed and baptized in fire, is frightening and painful. Those who do this will be completely transformed by it. The impurities of their hearts will be burned away, and they will become more wholehearted than they ever thought possible.

The fire of God burned so hot at Pentecost that its effects could even be felt in the city, even among unbelievers.

> *Then fear came upon every soul, and many wonders and signs were done through the apostles. (Acts 2:43 NKJV)*

God was present in His holiness. Even the enemies of God felt this presence and were sobered by what was taking place. They knew something unprecedented was taking place in their city and were completely unsure of what they could do about it.

Many churches today emphasize the baptism in the Holy Spirit and gifts of the Spirit. But if we look at the corrupted state of modern Christianity, we must conclude that we know very little about the fire of God. Many believers seem to have a small spark burning somewhere in their heart, but they are not "baptized in fire," immersed in fire, or walking in that fire. To walk in the fire of God is to walk in complete and wholehearted obedience.

If modern Christians were actually immersed in the fire of God, there would simply not be the sexual immorality, obsession with financial prosperity, fearfulness, and powerlessness that is seen in the church today. If we were truly immersed in the fire of Pentecost, that fire would destroy this corruption.

THE FIRE OF JUDGMENT

Not everyone was baptized in the Holy Spirit and fire on the day of Pentecost. The Pharisees and their entire religious organization rejected Jesus and were not filled with the Holy Spirit. Neither did they remember and obey the words of Jesus, when He said:

> But when you see Jerusalem surrounded by armies, then know that its desolation is near. Then let those who are in Judea flee to the mountains, let those who are in the midst of her depart. (Luke 21:20-21b NKJV)

The Roman armies surrounded Jerusalem in AD 70. Believers remembered the words of Jesus and fled. Those who stayed were slaughtered, and the temple was destroyed by fire. The Pharisees and their religious system came to an end.

And so the prophecy of John was fulfilled. Some were purified by the fire of God, and some were destroyed by the fire of God's judgment. Some were baptized in the Holy Spirit and fire. The trees that did not produce good fruit were chopped down and thrown into the fire. A harvest of grain was gathered, but the chaff was burned up and destroyed.

WE NEED THE FIRE OF GOD TODAY

The church today desperately needs the fire of God. We need the ministry of Elijah, who confronted Israel with the holiness and power of God. We need those who will confront the hidden sin in people's lives as Peter confronted the hidden sin of Ananias and Sapphira (Acts 5:1-10) and call our nation back to God.

We also need prophets who warn the people of coming judgment. This kind of prophecy seems completely foreign to the church today. Surely prophets are not to declare the Lord's judgments! Surely they are only supposed to speak good things, the things that people want to hear.

New Testaments prophets warned the apostle Paul that if he went to Jerusalem, he would be put into chains (Acts 21:10-11). New Testament prophets warned the people of coming judgments and calamities and told them how to prepare for them (2 Peter 3). New Testament prophets exposed sin

(2 Timothy 3). When Paul teaches about the gift of prophecy, he describes a church service in which unbelievers enter and are confronted with true and accurate prophecy, upon which they fall on their face, convicted of their sin, testifying that surely God is there (1 Corinthians 14:24-25).

American Christians have spent so much time and energy studying the blessings and goodness of God that we have forgotten He is holy and hates sin. We have forgotten just how much God hates the foul mixture of sexual immorality and idolatry Jezebel brings into our churches and our nation. We start to think that sexual immorality is not actually very serious and that all religions are basically good.

The Bible instructs us to study the goodness and the severity of God (Romans 11:22). We need both. We need to understand God's grace and goodness. We also need to study His judgments. If we do not, we become lawless and decide that God is just like us, supporting everything that we do. We need the ministry of those who have stood before God's throne, who can say as Elijah did, "As surely as the LORD of armies lives, before whom I stand . . ." (1 Kings 18:15)

We have too many preachers and prophets who have become skilled in telling people what they want to hear instead of speaking the word of the Lord. We need those who speak boldly and fearlessly the words God has given them. We need prophets and apostles who understand the judgments of God, who have studied God's judgments, who can warn our nation of what is coming if we do not repent. If we do not teach our nation about the righteousness of God and warn the people about the coming judgments, we will share in their condemnation (Ezekiel 33:1-9).

We need those who not only speak of God's judgments, but demonstrate them. Elijah declared that it would not rain, and it stopped raining. The messengers of God do not speak empty words.

We need the baptism of fire.

Chapter Seventeen

TAKING ACTION WITHOUT HESITATION

Elijah was a man of faith and action who won great victories over the forces of Jezebel. Despite these victories, Elijah didn't destroy Jezebel. When the opportunity came for him to kill Jezebel and remove her influence from the land, Elijah hesitated, and the moment of opportunity was lost.

In this book, we are learning about the spirit of Jezebel, not a physical woman. We are not talking about the use of physical violence as a way of dealing with this spirit. Nevertheless, we can learn much about dealing with the spirit of Jezebel if we study the ways in which the biblical queen Jezebel was dealt with. Those who struggle with Jezebel today must take advantage of God-given opportunities to take action.

On the same day Elijah called fire down from heaven, exposing the impotency of Baal, and killed the prophets of Baal, he was given an opportunity to destroy Jezebel once and for all (1 Kings 18). After the prophets were killed, Elijah went to the top of Mount Carmel to pray for the restoration of rains to Israel. Seven times he prayed, and after each prayer he instructed his servant to look for signs of rain. The first six times, the servant saw nothing. After the seventh prayer, the servant said, "There is a cloud as small as a man's hand" (v. 44).

Elijah then sent a message to king Ahab, "Prepare your chariot, and go down before the rain stops you."

The sky became black with clouds, the wind blew fiercely, and the rain began to fall. The rains were heavy enough to cause flooding, and it was only a matter of time before the road became impassable. The three-year drought that had begun with the prayer of Elijah was ended. Ahab mounted his chariot, riding swiftly to his headquarters in Jezreel, where Jezebel lived.

But as swiftly as Ahab rode in his chariot, Elijah was faster. The spirit of the Lord came upon Elijah, and he began to run even faster than the horses that pulled the king's chariot (v. 46). He was running to Jezreel. He was running towards Jezebel.

Elijah wasn't running towards Jezreel for exercise. God was giving him a short window of time, a divine opportunity to take action and destroy Jezebel before she even realized that her empire was crumbling. And so Elijah ran ahead of the king's horses like a man runs in a dream with supernatural agility and speed. It seemed his body could do anything.

Yet as Elijah approached the walls of Jezreel, he hesitated, deciding to stop and consider his options before entering the city. Elijah had outrun everyone else and now stood alone before the walls of Jezreel.

Was it really wise for Elijah to rush singlehandedly into the city in an attempt to kill Jezebel? Could one man really launch his own personal invasion into Jezebel's stronghold? Could he really charge the walls of the city without an army or even a sword?

Elijah had two options. He could enter the city alone and singlehandedly try to kill Jezebel, or he could wait for help. The first option required a miracle. Only God could give him victory in such a mission.

However, Elijah didn't need to rush into the city alone. The king was coming behind him. The king had witnessed the miracles of the day. The king had witnessed the fire that fell from heaven and the return of the rains that followed Elijah's prayers. The king hadn't stopped Elijah when he commanded that the prophets of Baal be killed. The king had obeyed Elijah when he told him to prepare his chariots to ride to Jezreel ahead of the rains.

Elijah had gained real authority with the king. By this point in the day, the king was actually obeying Elijah's commands. If Elijah waited for the king, he could use the authority he had gained over the king to invade Jezreel and deal with Jezebel. Elijah could perhaps work with the king to see righteous government restored to Israel.

And so Elijah waited for King Ahab, perhaps thinking they could discuss their next steps together. As he hesitated, the opportunity was missed. The king's chariot approached the walls of Jezreel. It didn't stop, riding through the city gates right past Elijah and straight to Jezebel's palace, where he rushed inside. As he did so, he left Elijah's influence and came back under the control of Jezebel.

Ahab gave Jezebel his report of the events of the day (1 Kings 19:1). He told her about the fire that fell from heaven, the return of the rains, and Elijah's command to kill the prophets of Baal. As the queen listened, a cold fury burned in her. When the king finished his story, she called a servant and sent forth her curse against Elijah as we discussed in chapter six. He fled for his life in a state of suicidal depression and terror all the way to Mount Horeb, the mountain of God (I Kings 19).

Mount Horeb was the place where hundreds of years earlier Moses had received God's law that Israel then broke so thoroughly. At Mount Horeb, the Israelites worshiped the golden calf while Moses met with the Lord (Exodus 32). When Moses descended from the mountain, he saw the idolatry of Israel. God gave Moses an opportunity to start over, proposing to destroy the idolatrous Israelites and create a new nation through the descendants of Moses. Moses refused this opportunity because of the covenant God had made with Israel.

Perhaps Elijah believed in his heart that Moses had made the wrong choice. The children of Israel were so hardhearted, so quick to return to their idolatry. They never repented for more than a moment. They murdered the prophets sent to them by God. Surely their evil deeds and idolatry proved that Moses had chosen wrongly.

Now at Mount Horeb, Elijah may have hoped that God would give him the same opportunity Moses was given. Elijah was ready to see the idolaters destroyed. He was so tired, so exhausted from their continuous evil. Elijah believed himself to be the only good man left in the nation. If God wanted to use the nation to fulfill His purposes, He needed to start over, perhaps by starting a new nation through Elijah.

Arriving at the mountain, Elijah climbed up until he found a shallow cave in the rock. There he slept, exhausted from his long journey. In the morning, he felt a voice speaking to him, "What are you doing here, Elijah?"

Elijah knew this was God speaking to him. He laid out his case before the Lord.

> *I have zealously served the Lord God Almighty. But the people of Israel have broken their covenant with you, torn down your altars, and killed every one of your prophets. I am the only one left, and now they are trying to kill me, too." (1 Kings 19:14 NLT)*

God said to Elijah, "Go out, and stand on the mountain before the Lord"

Elijah left his cave and stood on the mountain. Suddenly a great wind began to blow with unearthly force just in front of Elijah. The wind tore into the mountain and began to break the rocks to pieces right in front of Elijah. Elijah crept back into his cave. The Lord was not in the wind.

After the wind passed, the mountain began to shake. A great earthquake shook the ground on which Elijah was standing. Rocks began shaking loose from their place, causing great boulders to crash down the mountainside. The Lord was not in the earthquake.

The shaking stopped. A great fire began to burn upon the mountain, covering the mountainside with flames. Just as the heat of the fire became unbearable, the fire subsided and came to an end. The Lord was not in the fire.

Elijah cowered in his cave as these things happened. When peace had returned, he heard a still, small voice calling his name. Wrapping his face in his cloak, he came out to the cave entrance once again. The voice said to him, "What are you doing here, Elijah?"

Elijah repeated his complaints a second time. Israel was idolatrous and evil, and he was the only good man left. God then told Elijah:

> *Go, return on your way to the Wilderness of Damascus; and when you arrive, anoint Hazael as king over Syria. Also, you shall anoint Jehu the son of Nimshi as king over Israel. And Elisha the son of Shaphat of Abel Meholah you shall anoint as prophet in your place. It shall be that whoever escapes the sword of Hazael, Jehu will kill; and whoever escapes the sword of Jehu, Elisha will kill. (1 Kings 19:15-17 NKJV)*

LESSONS FROM ELIJAH

How did Elijah miss his opportunity to win complete victory on the day he defeated the prophets of Baal, restored the rains to Israel, and ran to Jezreel? How did he go from being such a decisive man of faith and action to being a man crippled by depression, fleeing from the curse of a woman?

The answer is very simple. Elijah took his eyes off of God and put them on people. As he did so, he missed the opportunity God was giving him. If Elijah had continued to walk in faith on the day he defeated the prophets of Baal, he would have confronted Jezebel in her palace with the same authority that he confronted the prophets. Jezebel would have died that day, and her reign of terror would have ended.

God didn't want Elijah to trust in the strength of man. It was God who gave Elijah the ability to run faster than Ahab's horses. God gave Elijah this strength so that he could finish the job. If Elijah had entered the city and confronted Jezebel, he would have been victorious.

Instead of taking that final step of faith, Elijah waited at the walls of Jezreel for the "help" of King Ahab. He put his trust in the authority of the king, and the king turned against him.

In the days ahead, God will give people of faith and action opportunities for victory. There are divine *kairos* moments in which God grants His servants great opportunities. Kairos is a Greek word meaning "right time" and referencing a specific decisive moment when conditions are right to seize the opportunity to accomplish a crucial action. Peter seized such a *kairos* moment on the day of Pentecost when he stood and called the city to repentance and faith in Christ. He seized another when he healed a lame man outside the temple and preached to the crowd assembled at Solomon's Porch (Acts 3).

The book of Acts is full of divine opportunities and confrontations in which the servants of God spoke the word of God with great boldness and demonstrated the power of God. In such moments, it is very important to put one's eyes upon the Lord and take the steps of faith He gives you to take.

Have you ever arrived at a moment when a step of faith needed to be taken and suddenly the whole thing seemed foolish to you? Perhaps God laid it upon your heart to take a step of faith in a certain area. Yet when the time of action came, you looked at the situation, and doubts arose in your heart. You became convinced that if you took the step you were intending to take, you would look foolish and your efforts would end in failure. So you backed down and missed the opportunity.

I can speak from personal experience of times when God told me to step up and publicly speak His word in settings where speaking such a word seemed very out of place. In high school, I felt God leading me to preach His word in my graduation speech. In college, I felt Him leading me to publicly declare His word to my college fraternity. There were times when I felt Him leading me to preach to crowds in the streets. There were times when He told me to risk everything to speak His word in settings that were dangerous.

Sometimes I obeyed. Sometimes I didn't. When I obeyed, I always saw the hand of the Lord. When I disobeyed, I always felt like I had missed a great opportunity.

We always have a choice to believe in God and take the steps of faith He gives us to take or to look at the circumstances and start doubting. In the case of

Elijah, when he took his eyes off the Lord, he missed his opportunity, and a door was opened for a flood of oppression to come upon him. He looked to mankind, and mankind let him down.

Then he started focusing on the great evil the people had committed in his nation. He became so focused on the idolatry of Israel that he stopped believing in his mission and stopped truly believing in God's ability to restore his nation. Without faith it is impossible to please God (Hebrews 11:6). Elijah gave up hope for Israel. Even when God displayed his great power, Elijah insisted that the situation was hopeless, that Israel would never change.

THE STILL, SMALL VOICE OF THE LORD

Why does the Bible speak of the terrible winds, fire, and earthquake in this scripture passage with the caveat that the Lord was not in the wind, the Lord was not in the fire, the Lord was not in the earthquake? Simply put, carnal men and women are always impressed with what they see with their eyes and hear with their ears. They are greatly impressed by extraordinary things such as fire, winds, and earthquakes.

Spiritual people are not supposed to be affected by such events the way carnal people are. Spiritual people are supposed to be led by the voice of the Spirit of God even when that voice speaks softly. Spiritual people know the voice of God. They are not impressed by other voices. They are not moved by events. Their actions and their view of things are determined by the word of God.

God desires to raise up people who can be led by His Spirit even when situations seem hopeless to others. He wants to raise up people who hear His voice clearly and don't care how bad a situation seems. Even when the wind blows and the earth shakes, they hold on to the word of God and are led by that word instead of being moved by the shaking of the earth or the blowing of the wind. They know that even the whisper of the Holy Spirit carries much greater authority than all other voices combined.

We are entering days in which everything that can shake will be shaken (Hebrews 12:27). The fires of God's judgment will rage upon the earth.

The winds of the earth will blow. Economies will collapse, and nations will shake. Many things that seemed secure and strong will be moved out of their place just as the wind broke the rocks and the earthquake moved the rocks. Multitudes will run to and fro in fear of these things.

But believers who know their God will stand. God is raising up men and women who will obey His voice even during times of confusion and chaos. They will not be greatly moved by great success or great failure. Even when the kings of the earth seem to respond to their message and turn to God, they will not put their trust in those kings. They will continue to put their trust in God and be led by God.

ELIJAH'S REPLACEMENTS

Elijah became so crippled by his depression and unbelief that he was no longer able or willing to do the work God asked him to do. So God told Elijah to go and anoint his replacements. He was to anoint Elisha as a prophet, who would continue prophesying to the children of Israel. He was to anoint King Hazael of Syria, who would bring the judgment of war upon Israel. He was to anoint Jehu, who would kill King Ahab's descendants and replace them.

Of course, it would have been much better if Elijah had done the work God called him to do. If Elijah had obeyed God and destroyed Jezebel, he would have likely succeeded in bringing the nation back to the true worship of God. It would not have been necessary for God to use Israel's great enemy, the army of Syria under King Hazael, to bring His correction to the land.

In fact as far as we see in Scripture, Elijah never actually obeyed God's instruction to anoint his replacements. When Elijah met Elisha plowing in a field, he didn't anoint him but threw his coat over him. In the end, Elisha did receive a double portion of Elijah's anointing after Elijah was taken up to heaven in a fiery chariot and whirlwind (2 Kings 2). Elijah never personally anointed Hazael to bring God's judgments upon the nation of Israel. Elisha had to do that (1 Kings 8:13). And finally in the case of Jehu, God also used someone else (1 Kings 9:1-6).

JEHU

After Elijah's flight from Jezebel, the nation of Israel continued in its idolatry. Years passed. King Ahab died, and Elijah was taken to heaven in a fiery chariot. First, Ahab's son Ahaziah, then his son Joram became king in Ahab's place. Because there was no repentance, the judgment of war came upon Israel. The armies of Syria under the leadership of their new king Hazael invaded Israel, pillaging and destroying.

One day the prophet Elisha told one of his young followers to find Jehu and anoint him as king over Israel (2 Kings 9). Jehu was the commander of the armies of Israel, serving under the leadership of King Joram, son of Ahab. The armies of Israel were based at Ramoth Gilead, where they were fighting the invading Syrian army. King Joram was not with his army. He had been wounded in battle and had gone to Jezreel where his mother Jezebel lived to recuperate.

The young prophet came to the house where Israel's captains and generals were gathered. He called Jehu into an inner room where no one could hear what he said to the commander. Taking out a flask of oil, he poured it on Jehu's head, then pronounced the message Elisha had given him.

> *Thus says the LORD God of Israel: "I have anointed you king over the people of the LORD, over Israel. You shall strike down the house of Ahab your master, that I may avenge the blood of My servants the prophets, and the blood of all the servants of the LORD, at the hand of Jezebel. For the whole house of Ahab shall perish; and I will cut off from Ahab all the males in Israel, both bond and free . . . The dogs shall eat Jezebel on the plot of ground at Jezreel, and there shall be none to bury her."* (2 Kings 9:6-10 NKJV)

After speaking these words, the young prophet ran from the house before anyone could accuse him of stirring up a rebellion against the king. Meanwhile, Jehu rejoined his captains. One of the captains asked, "Is everything okay? What did that crazy man want from you?"

Jehu answered, "You know what kind of man that was and the crazy things he speaks."

The captains became curious about what had taken place and insisted Jehu tell them what the young prophet had said. So Jehu finally told them: "He spoke to me, saying, 'Thus says the LORD: "I have anointed you king over Israel"'" (v. 12).

These words worked like a spark of fire in dry tinder. The captains of the army all revered their commander. When they heard that the prophet had anointed him as king over Israel, they immediately came into agreement with the prophecy. They began to shout, "Jehu is king!" Some took off their coats and laid them on the ground for Jehu to walk on.

Of course, rebelling against King Joram was a serious step indeed, one that could lead to the deaths of the conspirators if they weren't careful. Jehu understood the seriousness of what was happening. He didn't want word of the rebellion to spread to King Joram and Jezebel in Jezreel. If word came to them, King Joram could mobilize his forces to crush the rebellion.

Jehu ordered his captains to lock the gates of the city of Ramoth Gilead where they were based so that no one could escape to bring word to King Joram that his commander was leading a rebellion against him. The gates were locked, and Jehu gathered his men. When he was ready, Jehu set off on his chariot, riding at a furious pace towards Jezreel.

In Jezreel, a watchman in one of the towers saw a large group of men approaching the city. When the watchman brought the news to King Joram, the king was concerned. He immediately sent one of his horsemen to ride out to inquire what the intentions were of this approaching company. When the horseman drew close to Jehu and his men, the messenger called out, "Thus says the king: Is it peace?" (v. 19).

Jehu answered the messenger, "What have you to do with peace? Turn around and follow me" (v. 20).

Instead of returning to give his report to King Joram, the messenger joined Jehu and his men. Together they continued riding towards Jezreel. The watchman at Jezreel reported to Joram that their messenger wasn't coming back. Joram ordered another horseman to be sent. This messenger asked Jehu the same question, and Jehu gave the same answer.

The watchman reported to King Joram that the second messenger was also not returning. He told the king that the leader of the approaching company appeared to be Jehu, commander of the army of Israel, because he was driving his chariot in the furious manner for which Jehu had become known.

When Joram heard that his own commander might be approaching the city, he decided to go out and meet his men. Mounting his chariot, he rode out together with King Ahaziah of Judah to meet the approaching men. When he saw that the leader of the approaching group was indeed Jehu, he cried out, "Is it peace, Jehu?"

The chariots and men had all come to a halt on the very plot of ground that Ahab had stolen from Naboth. Jehu answered the king, "What peace, as long as the harlotries of your mother Jezebel and her witchcraft are so many?"

Now Joram realized what was happening. A rebellion against his authority was taking place. He cried out to his companion, King Ahaziah of Judah, "Treachery, Ahaziah!"

It was too late. Jehu drew his bow. As Joram turned to flee, Jehu released an arrow that sank into the king's back. The king slumped down in his chariot, fatally wounded. King Ahaziah managed to flee with Jehu's men in hot pursuit. He too soon fell to their arrows.

And so Jehu killed his king and took his place. Jehu commanded his second-in-command Bidkar to pick up Jehu's body and throw it into the field Ahab had stolen from Naboth the Jezreelite, reminding him:

> *For remember, when you and I were riding together behind Ahab his father, that the Lord laid this burden upon him: "Surely I saw yesterday the blood of Naboth and the blood of his sons," says the Lord, "and I will repay you in this plot," says the Lord. Now therefore, take and throw him on the plot of ground, according to the word of the Lord. (2 Kings 9:25-26 NKJV)*

Jehu and his company then entered the city of Jezreel. When Jezebel heard the news of what had happened, she prepared herself to meet Jehu. He rode up to her dwelling place, which was part of the citadel wall. Jezebel appeared at a window high up in the citadel, dressed in her finest. With all the dignity and authority she could muster, she called out to Jehu, "Is that you, Zimri, murderer of your master?" With these words, Jezebel compared Jehu to Zimri, a well-known traitor.

Jehu didn't even respond to Jezebel. Looking past her to where he could see servants standing behind her in the room, he called out, "Who is on my side?"

Several of the servants stepped forward. Jehu commanded them, "Throw her down."

The servants obediently picked up Jezebel and threw her out the window. Jezebel's body fell to the ground, her blood splattering the wall. Jehu and his men rode their horses over her body and entered the citadel, where they began eating and drinking, celebrating their victory.

After a while, Jehu ordered his men to properly dispose of Jezebel's body, saying, "Go now and bury this accursed woman, for she was a king's daughter" (v. 34).

But when his men went to collect the body, they discovered that dogs had already eaten Jezebel. Only her skull, feet, and the palms of her hands remained. This fulfilled the words of Elijah, who had prophesied:

> *On the plot of ground at Jezreel dogs shall eat the flesh of Jezebel; and the corpse of Jezebel shall be as refuse on the surface of the field, in the plot at Jezreel, so that they shall not say, "Here lies Jezebel." (2 Kings 9:36b-37)*

In this way, the rule of Jezebel and Ahab came to an end. King Jehu slaughtered all the descendants of King Ahab. He destroyed the temple of Baal and killed the remaining priests of Baal.

GOD'S JUDGMENTS ARE CONNECTED TO MEN OF ACTION

In the story of Jehu, we see a man who grabbed his God-given opportunity in a way that Elijah did not. Elijah was given supernatural strength to run ahead of Ahab's chariot to Jezebel's palace, before anyone could bring Jezebel the news of Elijah's victory at Mount Carmel. Likewise, Jehu rode his chariot like a madman to get to Jezebel before anyone could bring word to her of his plans. But when they came to the gates of Jezreel, Elijah hesitated while Jehu did not. Elijah listened to the curse of Jezebel, and the curse came upon him. Jehu did not speak with Jezebel or listen to anything that she said.

God is ready to punish all disobedience when our obedience is complete. He is ready to judge Jezebel, but first His people must be obedient, not just in their personal lives but also in the steps of faith He commands them to take. God's judgments are not released in a vacuum. They are released as His people take action and obey His voice.

We must stop being intimidated by Jezebel. Her authority does not come from God, and it should not be respected. The servants of God need to rise up and confront her wherever she is. We must confront her evil value system, her false morality.

We must stop pretending that sexual perversion is a good thing. Christians are so intimidated by Jezebel that they are unwilling to confront the flood of sexual immorality, homosexuality, transgenderism, and other perversity for what it is. It is an abomination in the sight of God.

American Christians are so desperate to be liked, to be accepted in American society, that we compromise our values. We try to live at peace with Jezebel without confronting her perversion and witchcraft even as she hijacks our schools, churches, and nation.

There are key moments when action must be taken. For every church that is hijacked by Jezebel, there was a time when those in authority could have confronted Jezebel and driven her out. There were key moments when those in authority could have refused to turn their school over to teachers controlled by Jezebel. May God give those who are on the front lines of our nation's war with Jezebel grace to recognize these *kairos* moments when action needs to be taken.

There is no such thing as peace when Jezebel rules a nation. Bondage and slavery are not peace. As Jehu said to Joram when asked if he came in peace, "What peace, as long as the harlotries of your mother Jezebel and her witchcraft are so many?"

How can there be peace when Jezebel is training our children and destroying our nation? How can there be peace as she tries to dominate every corner of society?

Peace comes when Jezebel is removed from her position of authority and influence in our land.

Chapter Eighteen

EFFECTIVE TESTIMONY AGAINST JEZEBEL

The primary weapon given to God's servants to use against Jezebel and other evil spiritual beings is the sword of the Spirit, the word of God. The saints overcome by the word of their testimony. But what kind of testimony is effective against Jezebel?

In this chapter, we will look at the kind of testimony that is effective in combating the spirit of Jezebel. But let's first examine the kind of testimony that is completely ineffective.

INEFFECTIVE TESTIMONY

Jezebel loves to draw people into ineffective, unfruitful conversation and dialogue. I grew up in the Mennonite Church, a denomination that valued dialogue, discussion, and mediation. When Jezebel began to bring her deception into the denomination, "listening committees" were set up to give her representatives a platform to share their views.

My father, a tenured professor at Penn State Hershey Medical Center and a Mennonite bishop, was involved in these discussions. During the 1980s, he began speaking and writing about homosexuality. In the mid-1980s, he helped the church develop its official position that premarital, extramarital, and homosexual sexual behavior were sin.

This was all well and good. The official position adopted by the Mennonite Church was biblical. Nevertheless, the church left the door open for dialogue on the topic. They formed a listening committee so that gays and lesbians who disagreed with the official church policy could be heard. My father was a member of this listening committee. At the same time, he was speaking on the issue of homosexuality in various conferences and colleges, often to standing-room-only crowds.

In the early 1990s, denominational leaders asked my father to resign from the listening committee. They said gays and lesbians didn't feel safe discussing their views to the listening committee because of the stand my father had taken publicly on these issues. My father refused to resign, but eventually the committee was reconstituted, and he was taken off of it.

So the conversation with gays and lesbians continued. Every voice that held to the official church position on sexual morality was sidelined and eventually removed from the discussion. Gradual compromises were made. The disciples of Jezebel gained a foothold in the educational institutions of the Mennonite Church and eventually in the administrative positions of the denomination itself. Thirty years later, the Mennonite Church is almost unrecognizable from what it once was.

When the Supreme Court ruled in favor of gay marriage in 2015 (Obergefell v. Hodges), the largest Mennonite educational institutions quickly changed their policies. They immediately added "sexual orientation" to their nondiscrimination policies and declared their willingness to hire staff and faculty who were part of same-sex marriages. They left the Council for Christian Colleges and Universities (CCCU), of which they were founding members. The CCCU represented one hundred eighteen schools in the United States, most of which endeavor to uphold traditional Christian teachings on sexuality and marriage.

The largest Mennonite denominational organization, Mennonite Church USA, is now in rapid decline. The biblical evangelical understanding of Scripture has been largely rejected in its educational institutions. Hundreds of churches are leaving the denomination as they seek to associate themselves with churches that actually believe the Bible.

TALKING TO JEZEBEL

Throughout the biblical accounts of confrontations with Jezebel, there is a common thread. The servants of God are repeatedly warned not to involve themselves in discussion and dialogue with Jezebel.

This can be seen in the story of Elijah, who ran to the walls of Jezreel so that Jezebel could be dealt with before the king came under her influence. When Elijah's hesitation allowed the king to meet with Jezebel, her words quickly brought the king back under her control.

This can also be seen in the story of Jehu when he arrived in Jezreel (2 Kings 9:30-33). When Jezebel addressed him, he simply spoke to her servants and ordered them to throw Jezebel from the citadel wall.

This can be seen as well in Christ's rebuke of the church of Thyatira. This church was rebuked for tolerating the ministry of Jezebel, who teaches, seduces, and prophesies, and for giving her a platform in the church to share her views (Revelation 2:19-20).

The danger of the wrong kind of dialogue can be seen in the story of the temptation of Eve in the Garden of Eden. When Satan approached Eve in the garden, he involved her in a discussion about the truthfulness of God's word with the question: "Did God really say . . .?" (Genesis 3:1).

Some kinds of dialogue are destructive and flawed from the start. When you involve yourself in discussions with those who are trying to twist Scripture to justify sexual sin, you are wasting your time at best and compromising at worst. Jezebel uses such discussions to try to stir up doubts regarding the Word of God. Those involved in sexual sin need to be called to repentance rather than debating with them the meaning of specific scriptures.

God's standards of righteousness are not up for debate. Humans cannot invalidate God's standards of righteousness by proposing their own standards or by sharing their own opinions about what should be right or wrong. We can only decide whether to rebel against God's righteousness or accept it.

The Word of God needs to be preached, declared, memorized, and believed. Open discussions and dialogue are useful with people who are actually seeking truth and willing to submit to the truth. They are not the answer for those who are attempting to evade the truth and justify sin.

So if dialogue with Jezebel is not effective, what kind of testimony is effective?

EFFECTIVE TESTIMONY AGAINST JEZEBEL

Effective testimony against Jezebel reveals the holiness of God, the judgments of God, and the greatness of God. Elijah testified effectively against the idolatry of Jezebel when he prayed that it would not rain, and it didn't rain for three years. This miraculous answer to prayer was a testimony to the nation that God is the Judge and that He would not accept the idolatry and immorality of Israel and Jezebel. Elijah's testimony proved that mankind's sin would be judged by God.

Elijah testified effectively when he called fire down from heaven. In this testimony, he demonstrated that God is real and that His power is much greater than the power of Baal. He demonstrated to the people that they needed to fear God, not Baal.

Another form of effective testimony against Jezebel is found in Naboth, who testified that he was not willing to abdicate his God-given assignment as caretaker of the land divinely allocated to his family even when his life was on the line (1 Kings 21:3). Naboth testified by his actions that his God-given assignment was more important than his own life. Everyone who stands firm in their God-given assignment in the face of Jezebel's attack gives similar testimony.

None of these testimonies involved discussions with Jezebel. None of these testimonies gave her the opportunity to try to make her own judgments and opinions equal with those of Yahweh.

In my book *Open Heavens: A Biblical Guide to High-Level Spiritual Warfare*, I tell the story of my sister's testimony against Jezebel that took place in our hometown in Pennsylvania.

A businessman in my hometown I will call Bob had developed a beautiful event facility on his property. It became a popular wedding venue, and some homosexual couples began asking to book the facility for their marriage ceremonies. A committed Christian, Bob refused to open his property for gay weddings. When certain groups learned of his "non-inclusive" stance, they began pushing for a boycott of Bob's business.

Bob tried to make it clear that he welcomes everyone into his business but was simply unwilling to offer his facilities for a wedding ceremony that went against everything he believed in. This wasn't good enough for the protesters, who decided to hold an LGBT rally in the center of our town. My sister and a group of other Christians gathered at the rally location to pray and stand in support of Bob. She later wrote the following report about the event.

MY SISTER'S EXPERIENCE

Something was rising in me as though like David I'd been given a sling and stone and was supposed to use it. I didn't know exactly where the protesters were assembling. But I felt God leading me to go to the town's square before our group's scheduled time to meet and worship at a specific spot in front of a café there.

It had dawned on me that the news media would be there, and I felt that the spirit behind the media would be an intimidating, angry, even murderous one.

I arrived at the square with my guitar and began singing praise to Jesus. A short time later, other Christians arrived. One brought his own guitar. Together we sang song after song of worship. Others of our group began praying.

At 11 a.m., the LGBT protesters began arriving. They became confused when they saw our group as they thought we must be the intended gathering point. Though their actual planned location was across the street, they decided to set up camp right beside us. They began waving signs with slogans like "Love is love."

The police were there too and various news teams. One LGBT activist had a megaphone to address the twenty-five or so protestors who had gathered. At one point, a protestor asked irately, "Can you stop singing for a while? We can't even hear what he's saying."

My people-pleasing nature wanted to accommodate her, but I knew in my spirit I couldn't stop, so I kept praising God in song. Someone put a camera right in my face. News teams spoke with various members of our group. I was thankful I didn't have to speak. We worshipped with one song after another until around noon when the crowd began to disperse.

When I went home, I felt God cautioning me not to watch the news or read about the rally in a newspaper. This was a relief since I had no desire to do so. I was just grateful I could slip in, do what God told me to do, and slip out.

My face did end up in the newspaper and on the news, but I made no effort to find out what people had said. One sister asked me later how I'd felt when one person got right in my face and yelled at me, "RUDE, RUDE, RUDE!!!" I had no memory of this and was grateful God had evidently protected me from things so that I wasn't even aware of them.

WORSHIP AMIDST JEZEBEL'S SERVANTS

After her experience with the LGBT rally, my sister and her husband felt God leading them to follow up with a different kind of public testimony. They began setting up a tent once a week along the main street in our town, where they worshiped and ministered to people walking along the street.

On one occasion, they prayed with a woman who was struggling with lesbianism. As they prayed for her, the woman broke down in tears and began pouring out her heart to God. "Jesus, I love You! I miss You."

My sister's testimony involved worship of God in the midst of Jezebel's servants. As she worshiped, she testified that God's authority is the real authority and that all the shrieking of the prophets of Baal was meaningless.

I believe that my sister's testimony had an impact on the spiritual atmosphere of our town. For years, a friend of mine had tried to organize public prayer and worship events in our town without much success. But recently, things seem to have changed. When I visited my home town a few weeks ago, I was amazed by all the spiritual activity that was taking place. A large group from various churches gathered in the town park every Sunday evening to worship God together. The mayor and police chief both participated in these meetings. Prayer groups were meeting in the park and other locations on a daily basis. I heard testimonies of salvation and healing as unbelievers in my hometown encountered the living God.

I am also seeing many believers in my hometown starting to stand up in the face of Jezebel. They are learning not to be intimidated by Jezebel's accusations and to speak the word God gives them to speak. Several friends of mine recently ran for the school board. They are using their position to take a stand against critical race theory and other initiatives of Jezebel.

I pray that one day I might move in a much more powerful level of testimony, the kind of testimony I read about in the book of Acts. I pray that one day I might preach with the same anointing demonstrated by Peter on the day of Pentecost when men's hearts were cut by the word of God, causing them to cry out, "What shall we do?" I pray that the fear of the Lord would once again come upon every soul as our cities receive the testimony that God is holy and that our only hope is found in the blood of Jesus.

Until that day, I want to be faithful to speak the word God gives me in churches, schools, and on the streets. I want to write the messages He gives me to write without compromise and take the steps He gives me to take. I hope and believe God will one day release that greater anointing, that His words will flow through me like a river of liquid fire that cannot be quenched. And of course, I pray this same anointing will be released upon all God's servants so that this world will know He is alive.

REMOVING JEZEBEL'S VOICE

As important as it is to learn to testify effectively, it is also important to remove Jezebel's voice from Christian organizations. We might not yet be able to silence Jezebel in the halls of power in Washington, D.C., but we are responsible to remove her influence from our churches, Christian schools, and other organizations.

The church of Thyatira was rebuked by God, because they tolerated the ministry of Jezebel, allowing her to teach, prophecy, and seduce. It is a sin to allow those who are influenced by Jezebel to teach in our churches, schools, and Christian organizations.

Jezebel creates a moral hierarchy with certain classes of victims at the top. These are usually people with unhealed wounds, with pain and bitterness in their lives that Jezebel can manipulate, turning it against her chosen targets. Jezebel gives these victims unassailable "moral authority" so that it is difficult to reject their teachings and their authority. They teach that those who hold positions of legitimate authority, white males in particular, are disqualified and illegitimate because of their membership in an "oppressor" category. They need to stay silent in the face of their moral superiors unless they are fully supporting Jezebel's initiatives.

UNFORGIVENESS

In fact, victimhood never conveys superior moral status to anyone. Victimhood is not a qualification for ministry, leadership, teaching, authority, or anything else. If one's victimhood causes someone to be filled with anger, bitterness, and unforgiveness, that should actually disqualify them from taking a teaching position or a position of authority in a Christian organization.

> *For if you forgive men their trespasses, your heavenly Father will also forgive you. But if you do not forgive men their trespasses, neither will your Father forgive your trespasses. (Matthew 6:14-15 NKJV)*

> *And whenever you stand praying, if you have anything against anyone, forgive him, that your Father in heaven may also forgive you your trespasses. But if you do not forgive, neither will your Father in heaven forgive your trespasses. (Mark 11:25-26 NKJV)*

Bitterness is unforgiveness. Those who desire to teach, minister, or hold a position of authority in the church must be free of bitterness and unforgiveness. They must forgive those who have hurt them.

This is very clear in the teachings of Jesus. Quite simply, those who do not forgive others will not be forgiven by God. They are disqualified from the grace of God and even from salvation itself. They are under the judgment of God because of the way they judge others.

FRUITFULNESS

It is fruitfulness that qualifies one to teach, prophesy, and hold positions of legitimate spiritual authority, not anger, victimhood, or membership in an oppressed category of humanity. The Bible teaches us to test the fruit of those who pretend to have authority in order to know whether they come from God or not. In His messages to the seven churches in Revelation, Jesus praised the church of Ephesus because it had tested the fruit of those claiming to be apostles and discovered they were lying about their apostolic authority.

> *I know your works, your labor, your patience, and that you cannot bear those who are evil. And you have tested those who say they are apostles and are not, and have found them liars. (Revelation 2:2 NKJV)*

Jesus commands us to test the fruit of prophets to know whether they are true prophets or false prophets.

> *Watch out for false prophets. They come to you in sheep's clothing, but inwardly they are ferocious wolves. By their fruit you will recognize them. Do people pick grapes from thornbushes, or figs from thistles? Likewise,*

every good tree bears good fruit, but a bad tree bears bad fruit. A good tree cannot bear bad fruit, and a bad tree cannot bear good fruit. Every tree that does not bear good fruit is cut down and thrown into the fire. Thus, by their fruit you will recognize them. (Matthew 7:15-20 NIV)

What is this fruit? First of all, it is the character of Christ, which is the fruit of the Spirit as the apostle Paul described in his epistle to the Galatian church.

But the fruit of the Spirit is love, joy, peace, longsuffering, kindness, goodness, faithfulness, gentleness, self-control. Against such there is no law. (Galatians 5:22-23 NKJV)

This fruitfulness is also seen in the transformed lives that are the results of a person's ministry and authority. A fruitful person disciples others in the ways of Christ, producing good fruit in their lives as well as their own, starting in their own households.

Those who wanted to be bishops in the early church needed to demonstrate good fruit in their personal lives. The apostle Paul gave a very detailed description of what that looks like to his son in the faith Timothy, whom he was mentoring as a church leader. This included good personal character, maintaining a godly household and marriage, and a good reputation among those outside the church.

A bishop then must be blameless, the husband of one wife, temperate, sober-minded, of good behavior, hospitable, able to teach; not given to wine, not violent, not greedy for money, but gentle, not quarrelsome, not covetous; one who rules his own house well, having his children in submission with all reverence (for if a man does not know how to rule his own house, how will he take care of the church of God?); not a novice, lest being puffed up with pride he fall into the same condemnation as the devil. Moreover he must have a good testimony among those who are outside, lest he fall into reproach and the snare of the devil. (I Timothy 3:2-7 NKJV)

In summary, this fruitfulness is about transformed lives. It is not about one's gifts, one's ability to speak or prophecy. It is about walking in obedience with God Himself and being transformed by the Spirit of God.

Victims need to be healed of their wounds and to forgive those who wounded them. Victimhood doesn't qualify anyone for anything. But those who have been completely healed of their wounds often receive spiritual authority in the areas in which they have been healed. The alcoholic who has been completely delivered from alcohol has authority to set alcoholics free. Those who harbor bitterness towards some "oppressor" group may be given authority to minister to those oppressors once they've been completely healed. They might even receive a deep love for the people they once hated.

FORBIDDEN TO MINISTER

Those who would presume to have authority in Christian organizations must be tested. The disciples of Jezebel must be exposed and their influence removed. They must not be given a platform from which to teach or a position of authority in Christian organizations. If the fruit of people's lives is not tested, we will continue to have our Christian organizations, schools, and churches hijacked by the servants of Jezebel. If they are not removed, they will always end up bringing the organization under the influence and ultimately the control of Jezebel.

Those whose personal life is a mess should not be given authority over others in a church, school, or other Christian organization. Those who feel resentful towards God's commands to repent of sexual sin should not be allowed to teach the Bible. Men and women who are living in bondage to pornography should not be allowed to hold positions of authority in the church.

Women who are full of resentment towards male authority should not be given positions of authority themselves. African Americans who are full of resentment towards whites should not be given a platform to teach or a position of authority in the church. Whites who are resentful towards African

Americans or other minorities should be forbidden to teach or to hold a position of authority in the church.

Those who use their victimhood to attack God's Word and legitimate authority should not be given the opportunity to teach. We need teachers who have something to teach us because their lives have been transformed. We need to listen to those who love the written Word, not to those trying to invalidate parts of it to justify sinful behavior or to ask, "Did God really say that homosexuality is sin?"

DIVERSITY

It really doesn't matter how diverse an organization is. What matters is whether or not the leaders of that organization are actually following Jesus. What matters is whether or not they have the genuine fruit of the Spirit in their lives. When we classify people according to race, gender, and victim status, we allow the door to be opened for the wrong people to take authority. This has happened over and over again.

This does not mean that only members of "oppressor" classes will end up in positions of authority in Christian organizations. In fact, organizations that set their focus on Christ and His kingdom typically end up having far more diversity in their leadership than those who focus on attaining diversity. God is no respecter of persons, and He raises up who He wills.

This can be seen in the Pentecostal movement that began at Azusa Street, Los Angeles, in 1906. In this movement, thousands of black and white Christians flocked to the ministry located on Azusa Street under the leadership of William J Seymour, an African American. There they waited on God together and were baptized together in the Holy Spirit.

I have founded several Christian organizations and ministries in different countries, and I have worked under the authority of different leaders and ministries. I have never intentionally sought to attain ethnic diversity in the organizations I started. I have always looked for those with the best fruit in their lives at the expense of other qualifications. Those who carry the greatest authority in these organizations today are certainly not predominantly white males. Neither are a majority of those to whom I submit my own life and ministry. Those I admire the most are those who exhibit the best fruit in their personal lives and service in God's kingdom regardless of culture, ethnicity, and nationality.

Just as one's victim status doesn't qualify anyone for anything, neither does education. Christians must recognize that America's schools are largely controlled by the spirit of Jezebel and that degrees from these schools don't qualify a person for leadership in a Christian organization. A degree from an American college or university does not qualify someone to become a pastor, teach in a Christian school, or lead any Christian organization. In most cases, such a degree should actually disqualify a person more than it qualifies them.

We must prioritize the fruit that is produced in someone's life over the degrees they have obtained. So many Christian organizations have been hijacked by people who seem to be academically qualified but whose personal lives simply do not display evidence that they have walked closely with Christ.

This does not mean we should be harsh with those who are disqualified. Even in Thyatira, Jezebel was given time to repent although she did not repent. Those under the influence of Jezebel are often wounded people who need healing, love, and patience from those who minister to them. Nevertheless, they should not be allowed to hold positions of authority or given a platform from which to teach until they are healed of their wounds and free of the influence of Jezebel.

Chapter Nineteen

STANDING IN LEGITIMATE AUTHORITY

The story of Naboth is about more than just an evil, oppressive system that caused a good man to be executed. The story of Naboth is about a man who stood in his area of God-given authority. He refused to surrender to Jezebel and Ahab what God had given him. When Ahab asked Naboth to sell his vineyard, he responded, "The LORD forbid that I should give the inheritance of my fathers to you!" (1 Kings 21:3).

When God gave the land of Canaan into the hands of Joshua and the children of Israel, the land was partitioned to the twelve tribes of Israel and to the families within each tribe (Joshua 13-22). Naboth's vineyard was part of this inheritance, given to his family by God. When Naboth said "The Lord forbid that I give the inheritance of my fathers to you," he meant it. He didn't think that it was right to just turn over to Ahab what God had given to him and his family.

Naboth was not a great prophet like Elijah. He had a very limited authority. Naboth was just an ordinary man who owned a vineyard. Yet he refused to abdicate his place of authority, his place of responsibility. He took a stand against Jezebel's evil governmental and religious system and refused to back down. One ordinary man holding on to his vineyard against Jezebel's entire system seems like an unfair fight. But in the end, Naboth's authority proved greater than all the authority of Ahab and Jezebel.

Naboth resisted unto death, and God honored Naboth's stand. Ahab's entire dynasty came crashing down on Naboth's vineyard, the place where Naboth had made his stand. A man's blood is not only in his own body but also in his descendants. Ahab's "blood" was in his son Joram. So when Jehu commanded his men to throw Joram's body on the plot of ground Ahab had stolen from Naboth, Elijah's prophecy that dogs would lick Ahab's blood in the place where Naboth had been murdered (1 Kings 21:19) was fulfilled.

If Naboth had submitted to Ahab's request and sold his vineyard, do you think Ahab's dynasty would been destroyed on his little vineyard? God is not only looking for people to take decisive, aggressive action like Jehu. He is also looking for men and women like Naboth who will simply stand in their area of God-given authority by refusing to give to Jezebel what God has put in their hands. He will be with them in their stand as the prophet Hanani promised King Asa of Judah when he was facing a great hostile army.

> For the eyes of the LORD run to and fro throughout the whole earth, to show Himself strong on behalf of those whose heart is loyal to Him. (2 Chronicles 16:9 NKJV)

They may not personally seem to win the fight with Jezebel as Naboth seemed to lose when he was murdered by Jezebel. But God will honor their stand, and He Himself will win the fight for them by bringing judgment upon Jezebel.

DIFFERENT ASSIGNMENTS

When God met with Elijah on Mount Horeb, He instructed Elijah to anoint Elisha as prophet, Jehu as king of Israel, and Hazael as king of Syria in order to continue the fight against Jezebel. In this commissioning, we can see the different kinds of assignments God gives to His servants and the different kinds of authority He releases to mankind.

God instructed Elijah to anoint Hazael as king of Syria. This might seem odd considering that Syria was an enemy of Israel and Hazael ended up leading

Syria's armies in battle against Israel. In fact, the Bible contains numerous instances in which God used Israel's enemies to fulfill His purposes by bringing His judgments to Israel.

Sometimes God will even use our nation's enemies for our benefit. He will use our enemies to humble our nation so we will return to Him. This is not His first choice, but sometimes the hardness of hearts makes it necessary.

Others are given spiritual assignments such as God gave Elisha and Elijah. The weapon they are given is the sword of the Spirit, the word of God. These people are not given civil authority in the governments of cities and nations but spiritual authority. They are commissioned to speak the word of the Lord and call people to repentance. They overcome by the blood of the Lamb, the word of their testimony, and by not loving their lives unto death.

God also gives political assignments as He did to Jehu. Jehu was called by God to take a place of political authority by becoming king of Israel. Likewise today some are called to become God-fearing politicians, schoolboard members, police officers, and so forth.

Civil authority is not given the sword of the Spirit. Civil authority is given literal weapons, whether swords, guns, etc., in order to fulfill their God-given mandate. These are not the weapons the apostle Paul spoke about when he said, "For the weapons of our warfare are not carnal but mighty in God for pulling down strongholds" (2 Corinthians 10:4). These are the weapons of the kingdoms of men, the swords of civil authority.

These "carnal" weapons cannot bring forth the kingdom of heaven or change human hearts with the power of the gospel. Nevertheless, they are important. Paul writes of civil authority:

> *He does not bear the sword in vain; for he is God's minister, an avenger to execute wrath on him who practices evil. (Romans 13:4 NKJV)*

Civil authorities cannot bring forth the kingdom of heaven, but they are used by God to keep order in society by punishing evildoers. Even when evil men's hearts are not changed by God's Word, their ability to spread destruction is limited when civil authorities do their jobs.

The point is this. Every assignment that comes from God is important in the fight against Jezebel. Naboth knew what he'd been given by God, and he refused to relinquish control of it to the enemy. It is very important to know the assignment God has given you and to stand in that God-given area of authority and responsibility.

We need politicians who refuse to back down under Jezebel's pressure. We need school boards that refuse to allow Jezebel's teachings on sexual immorality to be shoved down the throats of the students. We need parents who stand in their authority by loving and disciplining their children. And we need men and women of God who stand in spiritual authority, calling our nation back to God just as the prophets Elijah and Elisha did. When we stand in our assignments, Jezebel is unable to rule our land.

NABOTH'S BUSINESS

Naboth's vineyard was not just a piece of real estate. It was also a business with operating expenses, workers, and profits. Naboth was a businessman.

Jezebel is putting a lot of pressure on America's business leaders. We need businesspeople who stand up against Jezebel's attempt to control the economy. The Bible recognizes the authority of a man or a woman over their own property. God is not a communist.

In the New Testament when the fire of God burned in the early church, many believers were consumed with a desire to give everything to the Lord. Many sold their possessions and farms so they could give the proceeds to those who were in need. Some Christians use this story to support different forms of socialism.

Yet even this biblical account actually supports property rights. New Testament believers were never compelled by a religious or governmental system to share their possessions. They gave them away freely without compulsion. This is made clear in the story of Ananias and Sapphira (Acts 5). Ananias and Sapphira pretended to give all their possessions to the church, while in fact they were lying. Peter rebuked them with these words.

> *Ananias, how is it that Satan has so filled your heart that you have lied to the Holy Spirit and have kept for yourself some of the money you received for the land? Didn't it belong to you before it was sold? And after it was sold, wasn't the money at your disposal? What made you think of doing such a thing? You have not lied just to human beings but to God. (Acts 5:3-4, NIV)*

In other words, the land and the money belonged to Ananias, and nobody could take his possessions from him. The sin of Ananias was not the fact that he held on to his possessions. His sin was lying to the Holy Spirit.

In Proverbs, powerful people are warned not to try to take the land of their less powerful neighbors.

> *Do not move an ancient boundary stone or encroach on the fields of the fatherless, for their Defender is strong; he will take up their case against you. (Proverbs 23:10-11 NIV)*

In the days when this proverb was written, most people were small-scale farmers working their own land. These farmers were essentially small business owners. The laws of God were set up to protect these small businesses. Nobody was allowed to take from his neighbor.

There is a lot of pressure upon businesses to conform to Jezebel's mandates or face lawsuits, extreme fines, confiscations, and other financial consequences. May God strengthen businesspeople such as cake shop owners who refuse to participate in gay weddings. May God strengthen business leaders who refuse to force their workers to undergo indoctrination in critical race theory and other teachings of Jezebel. May God help them to stand even in the face of financial persecution.

May God help those around the world who are facing the intimidation of Jezebel to stand in their authority. I am working in East Africa at the moment. There is a non-profit organization that is pressuring Kenya to teach the American version of sexual education in schools. This would mean indoctrinating every Kenyan student in gay rights and sexual immorality. They would be taught that good is evil and evil good. Now is the time for Kenyan pastors and leaders to reject this deception even when that deception has all the authority of the modern world behind it. Jezebel is trying to hijack every country just as she is doing so in America.

STANDING IN AUTHORITY

We don't have to win every battle. We just need to be willing to pay a price as we stand in our God-given authority. God will honor this stand and this sacrifice just as He did with Naboth. Scripture instructs us:

> *Do not take revenge, my dear friends, but leave room for God's wrath, for it is written: "It is mine to avenge; I will repay," says the Lord. (Romans 12:19 NIV)*

When God's people stand, they demonstrate their commitment to their covenant with God. They demonstrate to the principalities, powers, and evil spiritual rulers of our land that they will not bow to any idol. They give a testimony similar to that of Shadrach, Meshach, and Abednego, the Jewish young men enslaved in Babylon who refused to bow to the idolatrous religious and governmental system of the king of Babylon. When King Nebuchadnezzar threatened these young men with death in a fiery furnace if they did not bow down to his golden idol, they responded:

> *Our God whom we serve is able to deliver us from the burning fiery furnace, and He will deliver us from your hand, O king. But if not, let it be known to you, O king, that we do not serve your gods, nor will we worship the gold image which you have set up. (Daniel 3:17-18 NASB)*

God honored the stand of Shadrach, Meshach, and Abednego and delivered them from the fiery furnace. We serve a mighty God who is able to deliver us from Jezebel and her system. But even if we give our lives in the struggle against Jezebel, it is okay. If God is for us, who can be against us? Even death is not too high a price to pay in our service of our Lord, as the apostle Paul, martyred for his own faith, states so powerfully.

> *Where, O death, is your victory? Where, O death, is your sting? The sting of death is sin, and the power of sin is the law. But thanks be to God! He gives us the victory through our Lord Jesus Christ. (1 Corinthians 15:55-57 NIV)*

Chapter Twenty

THE RESTORATION OF TRUE WORSHIP

In this book, we have discussed the church of Thyatira, the church that struggles with Jezebel, the church that is most similar to the American church at this time. Each of the seven churches described in Revelation faces specific challenges and is given specific promises to those who overcome those challenges. Here are the promises given to the overcomers of the church of Thyatira, those who overcame the works and influence of Jezebel.

> *And he who overcomes, and keeps My works until the end, to him I will give power over the nations—"He shall rule them with a rod of iron; they shall be dashed to pieces like the potter's vessels"—as I also have received from My Father; and I will give him the morning star. (Revelation 2:26-28 NKJV)*

THE WHORE OF BABYLON AND THE DESTRUCTION OF JEZEBEL

The church that overcomes Jezebel is given power over the nations. Jezebel is the system builder who builds idolatrous systems over the nations of the earth. The one who defeats Jezebel, ruler of the nations, is given authority over the nations, replacing the control of Jezebel.

As we stated in chapter three, Jezebel can actually be compared to the Whore of Babylon described in Revelation 17. This woman sits on many waters, representing "multitudes, nations, and tongues" (v. 15). She fornicates with the kings of the earth (v.2) and deceives the nations with her sorcery (Revelation 18:23). She is called Babylon (v.3), the great city that reigns over the kings of the earth. This Babylon represents all the religious, governmental, and economic systems that are used by the evil one to keep the earth in spiritual darkness.

Revelation 17 and 18 describe in detail the fall of Babylon. Jezebel will be cast down out of her position of authority over the nations just as Queen Jezebel was cast down out of her palace at the orders of Jehu. The evil religious and governmental systems of this world will collapse during the judgments of the last days. The nations whose authority is intertwined with these evil systems will fall with them, dashed to pieces like a clay jar smashed against a rock (Revelation 2: 27). The Lord Jesus Christ will rule the nations with a rod of iron (Psalm 2:9; Revelation 2: 27; 12:5).

These are like the days of Elijah, who brought the fire of God's judgment and purification to an idolatrous nation. In the same way, the overcomers of Thyatira will arise during a time when the nations are being judged for their idolatry. The evil and idolatrous systems of humankind will come to an end. The false religions of humankind will be exposed. Multitudes will see the real face of Islam and begin to flood like a torrent out of that evil religious system. Communist systems will disintegrate. The satanic reality of humanism will be exposed. Everything mankind has trusted in will begin to crumble. Everything they believed to be stable will collapse.

As the nations and their systems crumble, the true church will rise in authority. The day will come when the nations actually fear and respect the church just as they did the early church. When Paul and Silas were dragged before the Roman authorities, they were called "those who turn the world upside down: (Acts 17:6). They were known as men who shook nations with the power of their words.

The church that has been purified of Jezebel's works will have authority over Jezebel. Like Elijah, they will declare the judgments of God and call the nations to return to God. And as the systems of this world collapse into chaos, the church will be there to offer salvation to whomever is willing to receive it.

THE MORNING STAR

As the kingdoms of mankind disintegrate, a light will shine. Our Lord Jesus Christ gives the morning star to the overcomers of Thyatira, to those who overcome Jezebel. Brighter than all other stars, the morning star shines in the eastern sky during the predawn hours before the sun rises. But this morning star is not actually a star. It is the planet Venus. Because of its position above the horizon, it catches the light of the sun during the late hours of the night while the earth is still clothed in darkness.

Jesus promises that those who overcome Jezebel will be given great authority to rule with Him as He judges the nations. And even as the nations of the earth are being judged, the glory of the Lord will shine upon His people. In them the following prophecy from Isaiah will be fulfilled.

> *Arise, shine; for your light has come! And the glory of the LORD is risen upon you. For behold, the darkness shall cover the earth, and deep darkness the people; but the LORD will arise over you, and His glory will be seen upon you. The Gentiles shall come to your light, and kings to the brightness of your rising. Lift up your eyes all around, and see: They all gather together, they come to you. (Isaiah 60:1-4)*

During this time of darkness when people don't know where to turn, the overcomers will arise and shine with the light of Christ. This will lead to the great harvest prophesied in Isaiah and many other places in the Bible: "The gentiles shall come to your light, and kings to the brightness of your rising" (v. 3; see also Revelation 8:9-10). Even as humankind's systems are collapsing, multitudes will be call upon the name of the Lord and be saved.

This is God's doing. As the systems of humankind are collapsing, His people will be increasing in strength and glory. During times of great darkness, destruction, and confusion, they will begin to shine like the morning star with the light of Christ. This will cause multitudes to turn to the Lord.

THE LORD CONFRONTS JEZEBEL

The systems of Jezebel trap people in spiritual darkness, confusion, and bondage. God judges Jezebel and destroys her systems because He desires to bring people out of idolatry and back to Himself. A picture of this confrontation can be seen in the account of the woman at the well described in John 4.

In this confrontation, Jesus meets a Samaritan woman drawing water from a well and asks her for a drink. Since Jews and Samaritans despised each other, the Samaritan woman questioned Jesus as to why a Jew would ask a Samaritan woman for a drink. Jesus told the woman:

> *If you knew the gift of God, and who it is who says to you, "Give Me a drink," you would have asked Him, and He would have given you living water. (John 4:10 NKJV)*

Jesus then explained that whoever drank this living water would thirst no more but that it would become a fountain of water springing up into everlasting life. The woman immediately asked Jesus for a drink of this living water. Jesus responded by saying to her, "Go, call your husband and come here" (v. 16).

The woman replied, "I have no husband."

Jesus said, "You have well said that you have no husband. The truth is you've had five husbands, and the one you now have is not your husband" (v. 17-18).

The woman tried to distract Jesus from her personal life by engaging Him in a religious discussion, saying, "Our fathers worshiped on this mountain, but you Jews say that Jerusalem is where one ought to worship" (v. 20). But Jesus refused to allow their discussion to get sidetracked.

> *Jesus said to her, "Woman, believe Me, the hour is coming when you will neither on this mountain, nor in Jerusalem, worship the Father. You worship what you do not know; we know what we worship, for salvation is of the Jews. But the hour is coming, and now is, when the true worshipers*

> *will worship the Father in spirit and truth; for the Father is seeking such to worship Him. God is Spirit, and those who worship Him must worship in spirit and truth." (John 4:21-24 NKJV)*

Though a Samaritan, the woman believed in the coming Messiah. She tells Jesus, "I know that Messiah is coming (who is called Christ). When He comes, He will tell us all things" (v. 25).

To her astonishment, Jesus responded, "I who speak to you am He" (v. 26).

The woman was convinced by what Jesus said to the point that she returned to her hometown and began telling everyone she met, "Come, see a Man who told me all things that I ever did. Could this be the Christ?" (v. 29).

While she was gone, Jesus addressed His disciples, reminding them of their mission, their spiritual assignment.

> *Do you not say, "There are still four months and then comes the harvest"? Behold, I say to you, lift up your eyes and look at the fields, for they are already white for harvest! (John 4:35 NKJV)*

A large crowd of Samaritans streamed out of the woman's hometown to see Jesus. They listened to His teachings and invited Him to stay with them two more days. Many believed in Him, telling the Samaritan woman who had witnessed to them:

> *Now we believe, not because of what you said, for we ourselves have heard Him and we know that this is indeed the Christ, the Savior of the world. (John 4:42 NKJV)*

In this account, we see Jesus confronting the sexual immorality and idolatry of the Samaritan woman and the Samaritan people. He exposed the fact that the woman at the well had already had five husbands and was currently living with a man who was not her husband.

He then exposed the false religious system of the Samaritans. The Samaritans worshiped on the mountainside at the high places. These were the same hill-top places where the pagan Canaanites had worshipped their Baal, Asherah, and other false gods and where idol-worshipping Israelites had continued the practice (Numbers 33:52; Deuteronomy 12:2; 2 Kings 17:11; Jeremiah 32:35). Sometimes they offered sacrifices to God and sometimes to their idols. But in fact, they did not know God. Their worship was nothing more than another of Jezebel's idolatrous religious systems, a system that bound participants in spiritual darkness.

After confronting the idolatry and immorality, Jesus brought the woman to the true knowledge of God, the true worship of God. He revealed Himself to the woman as the Messiah. The woman believed and brought the testimony of Jesus Christ into her city. Many Samaritans put their faith in Jesus Christ.

THE RESTORATION OF TRUE WORSHIP

This is a picture of the end-time harvest. The systems of Jezebel will lose their authority over humankind. Jezebel's idolatry and immorality will be confronted. As they are confronted, the light will shine. Multitudes will be brought to the true knowledge of God and to true worship of God.

Jesus told the woman that the Father was seeking worshipers who would worship Him in Spirit and in truth (John 4:24). This is the ultimate goal of creation—to bring humankind back to the Lord, back to the knowledge of the Lord, back to the worship of the Lord.

As we battle with Jezebel, it is important to keep this ultimate goal in mind. It's not enough to defeat Jezebel. Jehu killed Jezebel, but he did not bring Israel back to God. In fact soon after the death of Jezebel, Jehu became involved in idolatry himself.

There is no such thing as a vacuum of authority or of worship. Human beings are created to worship. We instinctively search for something to worship. Those who reject traditional religion end up worshiping sports idols, rock idols, or science. When the idol of self is torn down in America and the stranglehold of Jezebel over our schools and nation is broken, something will quickly replace what is missing.

As these systems shatter and fall apart, there must be a church that shines the light of God in the midst of chaos and confusion. There must be a church that brings the nations back to God in order to replace their idolatrous worship with the true worship of the living God.

Human systems will collapse and fall apart, but God will be revealed. Institutional Christianity will collapse like the other systems, but the earth will be filled with the knowledge of God as the waters cover the sea (Habakkuk 2:14). This is the final harvest, the restoration of true worship on the earth.